C000178480

TEMPUS
Oral History
SERIES

HATFIELD
voices
from the '50s and '60s

'The Swimmers' water sculpture by Ralph Brown in the Market Place, September 1962. It has since been relocated outside the swimming pool. (English Partnerships/Ken Wright)

TEMPUS
Oral History
SERIES

HATFIELD
voices
from the '50s and '60s

Compiled by
Ann Burke and Mary Corbett
with The Boomtime Group

TEMPUS

First published 1999
Copyright © The University of Hertfordshire, 1999

Tempus Publishing Limited
The Mill, Brimscombe Port,
Stroud, Gloucestershire, GL5 2QG

ISBN 0 7524 1689 8

Typesetting and origination by
Tempus Publishing Limited
Printed in Great Britain by
Midway Clark Printing, Wiltshire

The official opening of Queensway House, the Public Library and 'The Swimmers', September 1962.
From left to right: Ralph Brown (sculptor), Gordon Maynard (Chairman of Hatfield Development
Corporation), Sir Keith Joseph (Minister of Housing). (English Partnerships/Ken Wright)

CONTENTS

Acknowledgements   6
Introduction   7

1. A New Town, A New Life   9
2. Houses and Homes   18
3. Working for de Havilland's and Others   33
4. Shops, Shopping and Services   46
5. Family Life and Children's Health   58
6. Sunday Choice   70
7. Free Time   76
8. Schooldays and Moving On   92
9. Getting There   104
10. Christmas   117
11. End Thoughts   125

ACKNOWLEDGEMENTS

The Boom Time Exhibition of May/June 1998 based on an idea from Welwyn-Hatfield Library staff was the origin of this group. Co-ordinated by Sue Kirby, formerly curator of Welwyn Hatfield Museum, memories and personal experiences of the '50s and '60s were explored and presented as part of the celebration of fifty years of Hatfield New Town. As facilitators of the oral history sessions, and with enthusiastic support from group members, we believed there to be scope for a publication. The Life-Long Learning Centre, part of Continuing Education at the University of Hertfordshire, agreed to sponsor us and we thank them for making possible this extension of our work within the department in 1998/99.

In pursuing this project we have received immeasurable help from Chris Martindale and Ken Wright. Chris has now given her time and expertise to this group for two years; her professional help has been invaluable and her local knowledge an essential ingredient of the oral history discussions. Ken took on the job of photograph researcher and has co-ordinated the search for illustrations. He has also orchestrated the sessions where the group members have seen what has been collected and participated in discussions on suitability and selection. We wish to thank the Hertfordshire County Council Information Service for the use of Hatfield Library for our meetings and for a contribution towards funding some of Chris Martindale's time, and also St John's church at Hilltop, for the occasional use of their committee room.

Our thanks go also to Dick Busby and Brian Lawrence for reading draft versions and providing much welcome advice on the preparation of this material for publication, to Councillor Frank Clayton for his enthusiasm and warm support of the group, as a member in the first phase, and for his interest in promoting the publication, and to Caroline Evans for many hours of transcription.

We pay tribute to the work of the Development Corporation and the Commission for the New Towns (now known as English Partnerships), without whom none of our activities would have taken place.

Ann Burke and Mary Corbett

This book has evolved from the weekly meetings of some forty or fifty Hatfield residents during 1997 and 1998, initially set up to produce an exhibition in May-June 1998 celebrating the fiftieth anniversary of the New Town designation in June 1948. The exhibition was one of several events, which included a community play and the making of a video. During the past year, 1998/99, fifteen of the original members have continued to meet to prepare the material for publication. This book represents the collective work of those whose names appear as the Boomtime Group.

Those responding to the appeal for residents who remembered the years of New Town development met for two hours each week in Hatfield Library. Sessions began with a short talk, film, photographs or presentation, often by one of the group, but also from people who could bring an area of expertise to the topic, by virtue of their work, or of their particular interests. These sessions provided ideal stimulation for the memory, and we are indebted to those who came to the group and who have allowed us to use extracts from their contributions in this book. Discussion was followed by a cup of tea and much informal reminiscence. Members then separated into two rooms, the better to accommodate the numbers wishing to contribute their memories, which were recorded on tape. These were transcribed each week and the transcripts returned for perusal at the next meeting. What you read in the following pages has been selected from a wealth of memories and the remainder will be available for public use in the Hatfield Library.

Oral history is an account of the past as experienced by an individual, a spoken recall of events and patterns of living, a life course remembered through the filter of later views, beliefs and feelings. Each account is unique, every view of a particular past will be the experience of one individual. Collection on a one-to-one basis has the advantage of a clear focus on that individual experience. In a group, any memory is being constantly revitalized, questioned or reformulated by those of others. However, there are common factors shared by those who went through the same events and there can be a spontaneous response to some memories which negate the presence of the tape recorder for a while and defeat the best efforts of any transcriber. Thus the recorded and transcribed material can reflect only part of the re-lived experience shared in the sessions. Some members also took a tape recorder to the homes of people with relevant experience, or invited them to join a session, and parents produced the recorded schoolday memories of their now adult children.

Experiences of starting married life in parents' homes and the excitement of coming to a modern house were, for a few, clouded by the loss of close family and familiar contacts. The majority, however, having the advantage of available work, were able to take the opportunities offered in a town where each could make a contribution to the social, working and cultural life as it developed. They were pioneers in shaping a thriving community which contained all the idealism of the post war period.

In the editing process the preservation of the spontaneity of speech in a group discussion, has been an important consideration. However, there is some need, in the interests of a wider audience to ensure the flow and continuity of individual statements, as well as to capture brief references to factors which mark an historical event or social change. In the setting up of homes, for instance, the development of new technologies and the absence or availability of these to a wider population has been portrayed by a series of statements, under a topic heading (e.g. 'Washing' in chapter 2).

In some cases extracts are unattributed, either because the speakers wished to remain anonymous, or because the comment was seen as representative of many others. In some cases problems of recording and transcribing discussion have made the identification of the speaker difficult. However, the use of all material has been endorsed by members early in the process. Illustrations have been carefully considered by the group for their quality, and selected on the basis of the contribution made to the overall impression of the '50s and '60s in Hatfield.

It has been a privilege to work in this group, and we hope that there will be more opportunities of this kind for the people of Hatfield and the University of Hertfordshire to pool resources and achieve benefits from community projects. We hope that our pleasure in producing this compilation will be reflected in the enjoyment of the readers.

Ann Burke and Mary Corbett

CONTRIBUTORS TO HATFIELD VOICES

The following members of the Boom Time Group have contributed to this publication:

Jean Beadle, Audrey Paris*, Joyce Chapman, Shirley Knapp*, Frank Clayton, Barbara Latham*, Reg Coleman*, Brian Lawrence, Maureen Cowie, Pat Lewis*, John Deans, Michael Marlow*, Anne Dunkley, Jean Marshall*, David Dunkley, Barbara Morley, Daphne Elmer, Jim Parker*, Valerie Turley, Constance Schofield, Claire Figg*, Barrie Smith*, Jean Franks, June Smith*, Pat Glanville, Frank Vann*, Fran Higgins, Janet Vann*, Peggy Jones, Joan Wadds, David Kay, Daphne Westwood, Joyce Kay, David Willson*, Ron Kingdon*, Ken Wright*.

* indicates members of the publication group.

Additional material has been supplied by the following:

Jessie Axford, Teresa Brummel (née Smith), Alison Cowie, David Cregan, Jaqueline Glanville, Nicholas Griggs, Donald Hodson, Janet Howard, Diana Jennings (née Turner), Gerald Model, Lyn Pedersen (née Vincent), Barbara Palmer, Tony Palmer, Sally, David Parker, Bill Storey, Margaret Tyler, Denis Williams.

CHAPTER 1

A New Town, A New Life

Sir Harold Macmillan, Minister of Housing, officially opens the first completed housing scheme by the Development Corporation at Roe Green in 1952. The flats pictured are 16-32 Pondcroft. (Ken Wright)

Becoming a New Town

Hatfield had got major problems. We'd got all these thousands of people who'd come to work at de Havilland during the war. They used to travel in by rail or coach from London or other places. Many of them were living in digs with families, and nearly every house in Hatfield had lodgers in those days with their own young families living with them. The Hatfield Rural District Council, a very little, old-fashioned council, mainly run by the traders for the traders in this particular area, was way out of their depth; they'd no idea what to do to overcome this problem. But in 1946 with the New Towns Act, and the proposal to include Welwyn Garden City, they foresaw a lifeline, and they appealed to the minister to make Hatfield a New Town. The minister of the day, Lewis Silkin, came to Hatfield and had a look. He felt he couldn't make Hatfield a New Town on its own, but he did come up with the idea of joining it with Welwyn Garden City in a joint board, and that was what was set up: half the members from Welwyn Garden City and half from Hatfield. The first chairman of that board was Reg Gosling; the Gosling Stadium is named after him. He was a very prominent member of the Co-operative Party, and that was why he was made political leader of the Development Corporation.

The first priority was to plan a new town of up to 35,000 population from the original 15,000; secondly to build houses for the new families attracted to the town, to help build new industry; thirdly to attract key personnel, managers, employees, service workers in building, electrical construction and other professional staff; and fourthly to build industrial and commercial premises.

As new housing started to become available it was allocated on a priority basis to new industry, to help them to get established. Big advertising campaigns were undertaken by the Government to recruit people to Hatfield and the other twelve new towns surrounding London.

Frank Clayton

A 'Key Worker'

I came to Hatfield to teach in Cranborne Infants' School which was quite new; that was 1954. Because I was a teacher I was allocated a flat in Roe Green and I was in Meadowcroft. When David and I were first married we still had that: a two-bedroom flat with a very nice bathroom. My husband still says it was the biggest and best bath he's ever had in all the other houses we've ever lived in. From there we went to Travellers Lane in 1960.

Anne Dunkley

A House of Our Own

My husband got a job at de Havilland's, but I think the main reason we came was to get a house. My mother died while we lived there so we had to stay to look after my father for a while, and then my husband got this job at Hatfield. He was working at Stag Lane at the time. We came out here to

The living room of the Roe Green show home at 197 St Albans Road West in April 1951. The furniture, mostly in the 'Utility' range, was supplied by Tingey's and three other stores in the area. (The Design Council)

look at it and were absolutely thrilled – it was marvellous, you know, wonderful to get a house of our own after sharing all that time.

What We Left

We lived in Hanwell, just before the war started. The house we were in was a three-bedroom semi but there were five of us then. Later my mother had another baby, so it was a bit crowded. There were three girls and two boys and I had to share a double bed with my younger sister. My older sister had a bed to herself in the same room. My two brothers were in a room which they used to call a box room, there was

only just enough space for the bed in there. But it was quite a modern house when I think about it, because my mum had an electric cooker and an electric copper. It had a boiler which heated the water but we had coal fires. But the house we lived in before, at Haslemere, didn't have any lights upstairs; it had electric lights downstairs, I think, – unless they were gas. I know we used to go up to bed with a candle, in one of those metal things. My sister and I, we used to chew the candle grease that dripped off. My mother wouldn't let us have chewing gum but we used to chew that instead.

Claire Figg

Bath Nights and Candles

I came to Hatfield when I married in 1958. Most of my life had been spent in St Albans. We did not have a bathroom and we had an outside loo. But I did not feel deprived; bath nights were very special. The rooms of our cottage were very large by comparison to rooms in houses now. The landing was the size of the bedroom: it was our playroom. We had gas lights downstairs, but we went to bed with candles.

Barbara Latham

The Long Wait

I was transferred to Hatfield from Stag Lane by de Havilland in about 1945. I got fed up with travelling backwards and forwards so in 1953 I applied for some sort of accommodation. I heard they were building bachelor flats. Time dragged on; I was living then with my parents in a three-bedroom council flat on a notorious council estate in Harlesden in North West London, Curzon Crescent, built to re-house the slums. I met my wife and we married and to maintain our position on the list we had to stay with my parents, because working in Hatfield we couldn't get any priority to get a house. In 1960 we finally got a house on monthly rental. We got the largest three-bedroom house that apparently could be given to couples without children. It was quite small, and built by Bryants of Birmingham.

Jim Parker

A House After Six Years

I came from Harlesden. I grew up in Harlesden and then when I married we went to live with my husband's parents in Burnt Oak. And we were subsequently there six years. My husband got a job as an electrician here and he was eighteen months travelling between Burnt Oak and Hatfield before we got a house.

Daphne Westwood

Leaving Family Behind

For some of the mums who came out with their families, 'the New Town Blues' was quite well known and understood. There were lots of people who wanted to move back to London because they had left their extended family there and there was quite a bit of loneliness, mainly for the young families. I lived in South Hatfield and we used to meet up in each others' houses occasionally but there was a lot of unrest.

Daphne Westwood

Breaking the Bond

We had our parents wherever it was. But they also had brothers and sisters so that made the community, whereas when we came to the new town that bond was broken. We were the first really to break out of having the whole family round us. Our children have never had that family feeling round them; they probably had grandparents near enough to visit, but not to be part of life the whole time.

Parks we Left Behind

One of the things which struck me when we were talking about what we left behind, was that both in Harlesden and in Burnt Oak there were parks within walking distance. There were about five parks that we could go to, but when we came to South Hatfield there weren't any parks. The whole thing about the London parks was that there were things to do, places to buy a cup of tea and all that. My mother had the bandstand in the Grove at Alexandra Palace, at the bottom of her garden. You could watch people playing tennis. You know, there was always something to look at, whereas in a field, unless you're a bird watcher, there isn't a lot to see. There were lots of fields, but they were all barbed-wired off. The only way we could go for a walk was over to Welham Green, which was some way off. And we lobbied at that time, some mothers got together in South Hatfield, as we were concerned that the children had nowhere to play. We didn't get anywhere – the council told us that the green bits at the side of the road was the place for children to play! But that's one of my first memories, and one of the things we left behind, the parks.

Daphne Elmer

Claire Figg primes window frames on the Self-Build scheme at Cedar Road, summer 1959. (Claire Figg)

Claire's husband Fred is about to do some bricklaying on the Cedar Road houses, summer 1959. (Claire Figg)

Triangle Self-Build

We were living in Kensal Rise and saw an advert in the paper that members were needed for a local Self-Build Group. So we applied and were accepted. There was a lot of planning to be done, suppliers to be found, but the Self-Build Federation helped us with this. Also we had to find a building society to loan us the money and in the end it was the Co-op that backed us – it's now the Nationwide. We could not draw all the money at once; a draw could only be made once a certain stage had been reached, such as the foundations, drains, damp-proof course. All these stages had to be inspected before the next stage could be continued with.

There were many meetings at our rooms in Kensal Rise. My husband, Fred, became the foreman. The building began in Cedar Road on the Bank Holiday, August 1958. The men had to work twenty-seven hours a week. This meant working at the weekend and two or three nights in the week. This was on top of doing their own work; there was no time for anything else and holidays were spent on the site. It was hard on their wives too, especially if they had children, so there were a few drop-outs and also some could not afford it, so new members were found to replace these; some came from Hertfordshire. A draw took place as to who should move in first. Two semi-detached were the first to be finished. If you had a detached you had to pay an extra £50 for the bricks for the end wall. Mostly, the men came up on their own to work but in the good weather some of us wives came up. I remember coming up and painting the window frames with primer.

When anyone moved in they had to pay rent to the Group of £3 2s 6d. No one started their mortgage until all the houses were completed. When you first moved in there was just pink primer paint on the woodwork, but the ceiling and walls were emulsioned to colours of your own choosing. You still had to continue building the other houses but it was better because you didn't have to keep travelling back to London. All the houses had fitted cupboards in the kitchen and all had central heating. Most of us had solid fuel boilers or oil; most have now been changed to gas. All had parquet flooring in the lounges and hall, mostly done by Eddie Sanford. We moved in in March 1961. The building was all finished in 1963 when we started our mortgages. There are still eight houses occupied by original members, there were fifteen all together. If you had stainless steel sinks and coloured bathrooms then you had to pay extra for all that, it wasn't standard. It was just enamel sinks in the original. Our mortgages were for £1,500.

Claire Figg

Dave's contribution

It was not only if you had a skill that you were able to join the group. Dave was in the print – he didn't know one end of a brick to the other. He was on the drains and he was very pleased with his work: he's got pictures of his first manhole! I was hod-carrying and general cement mixing.

Joyce Kay

Post-war House Sharing

We were just in rooms after we got married. We couldn't have a private conversation, we had to go to the nearest park which was Alexandra Park just to talk privately – you know, it was a horrible existence. We were four years living with my parents. It was a small house, it had three bedrooms and two living rooms. Our son had the little bedroom, we had the other bedroom. Our furniture was in store – it was in store for four years. It was pretty awful when we came to Hatfield, we got really desperate you know. We were sharing kitchen and bathroom.

Exchanging Homes

We put an advert in for Barrie's mother to exchange from a council house in Muswell Hill to a house out here. I put it in on Friday lunchtime and by Saturday lunchtime I had eleven people wanting to go back to London. I mean people did want to go back. That would be mid-Sixties.

June Smith

Going Back

In the late Fifties, Sixties, most newsagents and advertisement boards had 'Will you exchange from London to Hatfield?' for people trying to go back, doing a council exchange. And transport was a problem, shortage of buses, and not having a bus on Sunday.

Claire's house in June 1999 – she still lives there today. (Ken Wright)

Seeking Satisfaction

There was a considerable list kept in the offices of the Development Corporation for exchanges within the town. An awful lot of people very quickly decided they didn't like their neighbours or they didn't like the accommodation. I had a neighbour once who had been actually in seven houses in Hatfield. I think that showed considerable tolerance on the part of the Development Corporation. This family just did a couple of years apparently, or a year or so and then applied again; didn't like this, or something and so on.

Jim Parker

Journey's End

When I was born I lived in Kensington, then when the bombing became very bad I went to live with my mum, down with my gran in Leicestershire, then eventually my dad came down. Well we stayed there until the Japan war finished. When we came back of course housing was very difficult. We didn't stand a chance on the council either, so we went to live with one relative after the other until my mum and dad got furnished rooms. But I had to share my bedroom with them. Then I met Dave and we went to live in three lots of furnished rooms until we joined the Self-Build. That is why my home is my pride. It is very important to me, it is something which belongs to us.

Joyce Kay

An old folks' outing organized by the Oxlease Association, about to leave from White Lion Square, April 1965. (English Partnerships/Ken Wright)

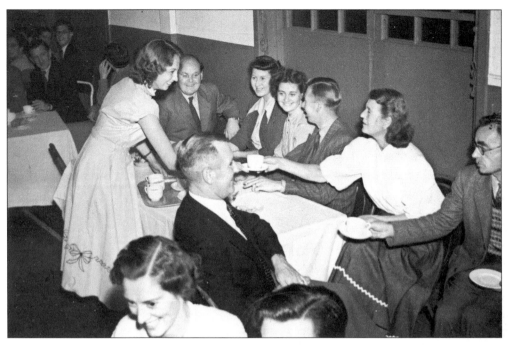

A welcoming party for new residents at the Fiddlebridge Club in 1954. (Buxton-Smith)

How to Get a House

There was an awful lot of fiddling going on with people claiming they lived in London, claiming they were married and all kinds of things. I had personal knowledge of a case where someone was having his mail poste restante to a house in Barnet and he never moved from Hatfield, and he got a house. That went on and I think it happened so frequently that they finally said, 'We want to come and see that you live where you say you live.' I don't remember if it was a male or female, but my wife and I had to be present and show them the bedroom and this is where we live. And the silly thing was, this was in Willesden, a town for which Hatfield was designated as an overflow New Town.

Jim Parker

Welcome to Hatfield New Town

There was a tremendous spirit then. You needed each other. After the Cavendish Hall opened there were monthly meetings called by the Development Corporation. Representatives of the different organizations were there for people who'd moved into the area in the last month. They were invited to come along so they could be told about all the different organizations.

Barrie Smith

CHAPTER 2
Houses and Homes

The southern end of Bishops Rise from the Garden Avenue junction, May 1956. (English Partnerships/Ken Wright)

Joining the Old and the New

That first house of the New Town was opened officially with all the VIPs there in April 1951. Bill Day, who was a councillor and also the District Scout Commissioner, took a piece of old rope and a piece of new rope, joined them together with a fisherman's knot and said, 'This is what it is all about, the joining of the old and the new.' For a long time, I don't know whether it is still, there was a frame up in the Cavendish Hall with the pieces of rope and the knot. The first houses were down opposite the New Fiddle.

Bill Storey

Moving In

I remember the way that people moved into the estate houses, it was very much a mixed group of people. You got teachers and doctors living beside people who worked for de Havillands, and people of all descriptions, because of the way people were allocated houses and happened to move in.

Donald Hodson

Ice Cream Counter

Our first house in Days Mead had what we called the 'ice cream counter'. It was a very shallow window in the lounge, set forward as a bay so there were four panes, but they were so shallow that you felt like you should open a window and sell the ice creams. The lounge itself was very dark.

June Smith

Housing the Pram

At the start of 1950 our family had just moved from a two-up two-down in Old Hatfield to a new council house in the developing Birchwood estate. The new house had a second WC, a laundry room, a workshop, fuel store and a large entrance hall measuring 8ft by 15ft including stairway. I recall that there had been much talk of pre-war houses being built with hallways so small that prams had to be stored in the living room or damp out-buildings. The post-war authorities were determined that their houses would have adequate indoor storage for the large prams of the time.

Reg Coleman

Modern Inconveniences

In 1957 we moved into a one-bedroom flat in Robins Way. We had no heating and no cupboards. In 1959 we aired the baby's bedding and clothes in the cooker. When we moved to Dove Court in 1960 we purchased a wardrobe, dressing table and lounge furniture. We had an old carpet from Mother. The neighbours upstairs had no carpet and so the noise was bad.

Jeannie Franks

The Ryde development: houses for sale in The Holdings are nearing completion in March 1962. (English Partnerships/Ken Wright)

Housing the Car

We moved into Bishops Rise because we had a car, so wanted a garage. It was very pleasant and we had nice neighbours. There was a green area in front. There was a communal drying room but the rain came in, so we dried washing in the bathroom. Washing could not be hung out. I remember the spin dryer was very noisy.

Barbara Morley

Houses to Buy

I moved in June 1965 on to the Ryde Estate. It was not easy to buy a house. There were sixty houses on the list then available. 16 Pleasant Rise was a detached three-bedroom house in a sixteenth of an acre, which we got for £6,350. It was a staggered row of houses which gave us privacy. The house was open plan with parquet flooring which was ruined on day one. We had gravel and it was a wet day when we moved in. We had an L-shaped living room and the sunshine came into the kitchen. We fell in love with the house. The architect and developer was from the Louis de Soissons partnership in Welwyn Garden City. The quality of woodwork was not good, there were bad joints so the paint wouldn't hold and rotting wood was also a problem. The paint was battleship grey throughout the house. We had to have specific colours, bog-standard colours. There were strong white 12in weatherboards. We had the house on a 999-year lease, although the terms of the lease are not enforced. It was built as an integral estate. There were restrictions on hedges, wires, posts, TV aerials. You couldn't keep chickens, horses, sheep, etc.

John Deans

Cooler up the Hill

In 1954 we moved into a house in Hillcrest. It was a three-bedroom terraced house which we monthly rented. There was a left-hand side cloakroom and toilet, a living room and a dining room on the right. On the right-hand side of the front door there was a storeroom with doors to the

kitchen and garden. Upstairs we had an airing cupboard, a toilet, a double bedroom with fitted cupboard, a second double bedroom with platform over the stairs, and a third smaller bedroom. We had no radiators, towel rail or fridge. We liked the house very much although it was cold. They used to say that as you went uphill the money ran out, so we didn't have central heating – only an open fire. We waved to people walking on Sunday who were looking through our rooms because the windows had unfrosted glass.

All Under Cover

Our coal shed was inside. The house had a double front and a side door that was the storeroom. The back of the

Bishops Rise, looking towards the de Havilland factory in 1953. Construction of the Roe Green shops and Cavendish Hall has just begun. (English Partnerships/Ken Wright)

storeroom was an under-stairs cupboard for the coal and it was jolly nice not to have to go outside to get the coal, except of course all the dust used to go into the kitchen.

A Heated Towel Rail

We moved in March 1955 and it snowed. It was 27 Bishops Rise, a three-bedroom end of terrace house. There were stairs in the front and the front room was on the left-hand side. There was a toilet and cloakroom. We had a through room with folding glass doors. We had a nice big kitchen with a side door to the utility room and a door to the garden. We had to carry things through the house. The bathroom was in the far right hand corner. The bedroom over the utility room was very cold. We had a bitumastic floor, a dark brown composition. The fireplace was on the left-hand side in the front room. We had an open fire and there was a stone shelf with cupboards underneath. We had no central heating but had a heated towel rail in the bathroom. The lavatory was separate from the bathroom. We had a big airing cupboard. The garden was enclosed on three sides. You could clean all your own windows from the ledge. There was a shelf over the stairs and in the alcove in the bedroom there were fitted wardrobes.

Janet Vann

Half a Crown for a Fridge

In 1964 we moved into Briars Close. We had a left-hand side lounge and a right-hand side kitchen/diner. The stairs went up and round. We had three bedrooms, one large and two small. We had a door to the outhouse and garden. There was a door on the outside which you could go through which had a coal bunker in it. I had come from a one-bedroom house, with kitchen/diner, in Stoke Newington where the rent was £2 7s 6d and our whole new house cost only 5s extra a week. We couldn't believe it! We had the fridge taken out because you paid an extra half crown for a fridge, gas fired.

Jean Beadle

Living in Roe Green Lane

The block of flats my wife and I lived in was at the end of Roe Green Lane, and it was filled with a very considerable mixture of people. The man who owned the cinema was part of it, an engineer from de Havilland's, there was me, and we felt a tremendous social mix and a tremendous closeness, without actually getting in one another's way. It seemed to me to be ideal, this happy, very democratic way of living. I remember there was suddenly a problem over parking. We weren't allowed to park our cars outside that block of flats because it was causing congestion. And I remember the whole block of flats getting together and deciding on a little parking indent there, and putting it to the Development Corporation and they built it for us and everything was all right.

David Cregan

Days Mead to Bishops Rise

We came out here, through de Havilland's having the list for engaged people and then for married people. I was all agog at what I was going to get, but was very disappointed in only having a two bedroom house as we only had one child and we were on Days Mead and watched Cavendish Way being built. It was a very interesting time and the Comet was running its engines so we couldn't have any windows open if we wanted to talk! The floors and bathroom and kitchen were much better quality than where we moved into two years later, in Bishops Rise. We moved there in 1954, and we've been there ever since. We moved there before there were any street lights or pavements, though we had a step down into our house from what was going to be a pavement. I was the first to move into the block of eight and it was a bit eerie because Barrie was away.

June Smith

From Weekly to Monthly Rental

We moved in December 1959 to 15 Garden Avenue, a small three-bedroom house. There was a stairwell in one bedroom with a platform. You faced the stairs as you went in. There was a kitchen/diner and you ate in the kitchen. There was no central heating but coal fires and back-boilers. We had no fridge. We rented the house weekly. In 1966 we moved to a four-bedroom monthly-rented house. You had to show the Corporation you could pay OK. There was a back entrance to the house

Children at play in Garden Avenue, April 1962. (English Partnerships/Ken Wright)

Janet and Frank Vann with baby Roderick at their first home in Bishops Rise, 1956. (Frank Vann)

and it had a long kitchen/diner, small living room, and downstairs toilet. I'm still living there.

Daphne Westwood

Rubble and Rotavators

We moved in in 1957. It was in Bradshaws, a just-built four-bedroom house. It had a curved staircase with a window on the stairs. The garden was full of rubble and it needed a rotavator. There was a porch, and an outhouse next to the kitchen which was large. There was a small hall, a living room with a coal fire and back-boiler. We had one large bedroom and three small ones, and a downstairs toilet.

There were seven children and homework was done in cold bedrooms. We had French windows and we put in sliding doors.

Fran Higgins

House Martins

When we lived in Hatfield first, we lived on Bishops Rise on the west side of the hill and we moved in July 1958 to Elm Drive on the east side of the hill and all these house martins were chattering. It was just lovely, you'd lie in bed, we'd got about four or five nests under our eaves. We had them year after year, and then suddenly they stopped coming. I understand it's because the

Sahara has become slightly wider from north to south and they can't get as far as here now. Occasionally I see them, I wonder if anybody has them. They were all over the Trees Area, weren't they, a lot of the houses around had them. They made such a mess on the windows, but I'm sorry they have disappeared.

Janet Vann

A Green-fingered Dad

I can still see clearly how my dad laid out that back garden, the steps he built. It was just all clay; he put two small lawns there and a path and a flight of steps, lushes of pinks along either side and then we had a vegetable garden at the top where Mum used to hang the washing out. But it was interesting all along the block how different people did their gardens and how some could afford to pay more for different things and others that couldn't. My father was a great propagator, a very green-fingered person. When I went to school you'd see what they'd done in their gardens. A lot of people had never had a garden before and what were they going to do with it? It was marvellous actually in Hatfield, thinking round all the estates everybody seemed to have a crack at the garden in those days whether they'd got knowledge or not, it didn't really matter, everybody made an effort.

Lyn Pedersen (née Vincent)

Lyn Pedersen in her garden in Holliers Way with her younger sister Patricia in 1954. The three Lee brothers visiting from north London were very envious of the girls' new surroundings. (Lyn Pedersen)

Garden Fun

Families used the gardens. They played in the gardens, they were full of the family.

June Smith

Garden Path

We had a garden just like that, a garden path with a line of posts 6ft on either side. When I started planning my garden there was no room for that so I dug it up, 4 inches of concrete. Being a righteous-minded person I went and told my Housing Manager at the time that I was doing that. He said 'You'll have to put it back and apply for permission to do that kind of thing. We can't have people pulling up paths that we put down.'

Frank Clayton

Corporation Controls

In Briars Close a family had put up a lovely sun room, beautifully built by the husband and fully glazed. When they moved they told the Corporation that they were leaving the house, and they had to take it down before they went.

The Development Corporation used to control the design of the fences. And what colour roofing felt to put on your shed, no panels were allowed to hold it down.

DIY was not allowed. We put plastic tiles in the hall and they were not really allowed. All the external paintwork had to stay the same.

Michael Marlow, Barrie Smith and another group member

When the Roofs Came Off

I'm in the middle of Robins Way, and it was when Stephen was a baby so it must have been in 1957 I would think, and Christine was three. We were woken up by banging on the door, and the police were there and they said 'We advise you to go down stairs because of the roofs.' Well, we couldn't believe this kind of thing, so we stayed put. In the morning, we had one end of the roofs on our garden here, and the other end on our garden there. Only three of us had our roofs still intact; they just lifted up and folded over, because there hadn't been any instructions for screwing the roofs to the beams. They were only done with three-inch nails.

Jessie Axford.

Thirty in a Double Bed

When the roofs came off they actually hit our front window, we just thought it was a bomb going off, something like that. My husband ran out and there were people just sort of looking, and children crying, and we just automatically said, 'Bring all the children up and put them in the bed.' Thirty in a double bed. The mothers were sitting in the lounge on the chairs, on the floor, and the men were trying to salvage clothes.

Jeannie Franks

The kitchen of the Roe Green show house, one of the first houses built by the Development Corporation, in April 1951. (The Design Council)

A Question of Saving Up

I managed to save up for a fridge in 1957. I told the head of the school where I was teaching so I could do a little bit more supply to be able to afford a fridge. It was a question of money and it was £70 which was a lot of money. It was a Kelvinator …it was a question of saving up in those days and it was a lot.

David Cregan

Identity Established

I got a loan from the Midland Bank in 1962. The only time I was ever recognized as 'Mr Smith', actually, was when I owed them money.

Barrie Smith

See the new

CORONATION "ADA"

Washing Machine with
POWER OPERATED WRINGER

at the amazing price of

50 GNS
TAX PAID

Hire Purchase Terms Gladly Arranged

Send for descriptive leaflet or ask our representative to call.

SYDNEY RUMBELOW

5 The Parade - HATFIELD

Phone 2828   And at Hitchin and Stevenage

An advertisement from Coronation year, 1953.

Scarce Credit

One time in my seeking a house, I had thought of buying. I had accumulated the ten per cent deposit for the particular house in mind and overnight the Chancellor decided one should have twenty per cent. My salary was being paid into the bank, but I couldn't get a loan or anything. They wouldn't allow wives salary, overtime pay wasn't counted, just basic salary.

Jim Parker

Conversation about Fridges

Shopping took a lot of time, because we had no cars, and without fridges and freezers, you were doing it more than once a week.

In 1960 when I moved here, I was working at de Havilland for £1,000 a year. I have two sisters and I was the only member of my family to have a fridge and a washing machine.

We had our own fridge which we bought in 1957 which was an Electrolux. It had a very small ice compartment, you could just get in a block of ice cream.

It was a great treat to have things like lettuce and tomatoes nice and cold and children's drinks, but they weren't very big, you didn't have much space.

Before we got a refrigerator we used the larder and some may have used the meat safe which was often fixed to the back wall on the shady side of the house.

Our houses had a fridge under the draining board, which you paid extra for in the rent.

Some of the early fridges had locks on them.

Peggy Jones, June Smith and others

Washing

Without washing machines it was a copper, and put your sheets into boil. Washing took a whole day, Monday was washing day.

I used to send my sheets to the laundry at Wellfield. They used to come and collect them. But I'd do the rest of the washing.

In 1963 we bought our first washing machine through a catalogue. You didn't have to put a deposit down and it worked out the same price as if you'd bought it outright. It worked out about 1s 9d a week.

Rolls Razor Washing Machines

In those days you could have something on approval for two or three days. I remember having a washing machine for a few days before deciding whether to buy it or not. I remember having at least three, one after the other over a fortnight which I'm sure they don't do now. The trouble with the Rolls machines was that the belt kept coming off. I think they went bankrupt.

John Bloom Machines

John Bloom was the man who took over the Rolls Razor company with a vow that he could put a washing machine in every British home. When we were contemplating our purchase I sent off a coupon in the paper. About seven o'clock one Saturday morning there came a hammering at the door and I looked out of the bedroom window and there was a fellow out there with a washing machine. I said that I didn't want the washing machine I just wanted to read about them comparing them with other makes and he said 'Its our policy: we believe you don't want to read about them you want to see it in action, we bring them to the home.' So I said, 'I'm sorry we aren't ready to see a washing machine demonstration, please take it away.' But it just shows how keen his methods were.

Jim Parker

Scandinavian-style

We had a problem with buying the right type of furnishings, probably

A Nathan Sideboard

There was G-plan; I've still got a G-plan wardrobe, a Nathan sideboard, Ercol chairs and two armchairs. I think that we got our first carpet at Times Furnishing in St Albans.

Clare Figg

Ideal Homes

I was married in 1963 and we went to the Ideal Home Exhibition and that's where we chose our furnishing. The furniture we bought was Nathan and Meredew and we ordered it there. It had money off because it was an exhibition offer. Things last – I bought a sewing machine for my twenty-first birthday at the Ideal Home Exhibition and it still works, but it is so heavy.

Pat Lewis

Floor Coverings

We had Cyril Lord carpet in our bedroom, I suppose because my next door neighbour, took on selling them. When we built the houses he was selling them. So we were all buying his carpets, Cyril Lord carpets. It did last quite a long time but it had that foam stuff on the back. It felt quality but it wasn't really. It was thin, very thin.

You still only had a carpet square, very often, and polished the outside border around it.

It was about this time that the broadloom carpets came in. Previously it had been made as squares or rectangles, but I remember one Cyril Lord advert

Shirley and Norman Knapp in her parents' garden in Welwyn Garden City in 1956. (Clifford C. Turnbull)

because we had an open plan timber house. We used to go up to Heals to buy furniture. It was very much the 1960s Scandinavian type which we still have; very dated now. It's very simple, teak wood. Our furnishing fabrics came from Heals as well and I think we liked it because we didn't like clutter and fancy bits and pieces and that's why we decided to spend a little more money and buy that type.

Shirley Knapp

claiming to bring luxury carpets to the people, as it were.

Our carpet was stitched: it was 27in wide and they brought it to the house and stitched it there. I always remember they'd got a young fellow with them who was just learning. The bit he stitched I didn't think was very good, you could see the stitches. It was Wilton so it didn't wear out.

If you couldn't afford a carpet you could buy carpet pads, of embossed plastic with felt backing; on the staircase it was terrible. It made a heck of a noise but it did do a good job. When I bought a Morris Traveller I lined the back end with it and when I sold it the back looked as good as new.

Nobody had their stairs completely covered; your stair carpet had a border of stair each side.

The first house we had in Days Mead the floors were the lovely black Marley tiles and the house in Bishops Rise was the composition floor which you just cover up.

Jim Parker, Janet Vann, June Smith, Claire Figg and others

Brushwork

I don't think I did have a vacuum cleaner when we first came. I used a brush and carpet sweeper.

I used to borrow one off a friend, lug it to my house, and try to do it all through.

I had a soft brush and a hard brush. And there were more floors with lino, so you needed brooms and brushes more.

We had parquet floors and I used to have a mop and polish.

Claire Figg and others

Local Producer

With Frank Murphy's factory at Welwyn Garden City many people got 'Home' Murphy radios.

Ron Kingdon

E. T. TINGEY & SONS (Hatfield) LTD.

House Furnishers, Ironmongers, Cycle and Sports Dealers, Removal and Storage Contractors

ST. ALBANS ROAD, HATFIELD, HERTS.

Telephone Nos. 3224/5   Established 1869

 1869   *Proudly Announce 86 years of Successful Trading in Hatfield*   **1955**

An advertisement for Tingey's in 1955. (*Herts Advertiser*)

ROLANDS

BROADLOOM FITTED CARPETS

ESTIMATES FREE

Plain or Patterned —
Any make supplied

LARGE CASH DISCOUNTS OR CREDIT TERMS

BUY NOW on our NO DEPOSIT Voucher System !

ON THESE TERMS YOU CAN AFFORD TO HAVE FITTED CARPETS

Examples: £50 only 12/- WEEKLY. — 100 WEEKS.
£75 only 18/- WEEKLY. — 100 WEEKS.
£100 only 24/- WEEKLY. — 100 WEEKS.

WE ALSO RE-FIT YOUR OWN CARPETS

12-13 The Parade
(OPPOSITE POLICE STATION)

and

St. Albans Road East Hatfield. Tel.: 63894

An advertisement for Rolands from 1967. They are still trading in Hatfield town centre.

Cat's Whisker

The radios we are talking about are all valve radios. I made a cat's whisker radio for our daughter and she had it in her bedroom with headphones.

Frank Vann

DIY Sound Systems

If you wanted quality reproduction in those days you could actually buy kits. Mullard, the electrical company, made a kit of a famous amplifier and one bought this and assembled it. I believe several firms did this and you could get it by post, Wharfedale speakers for example. You put this into the box and lined the box with foam or whatever. We had an Ultra that was in the contemporary sense just a light wood coffin on black matt legs. We bought that from a shop in Welwyn Garden City.

Jim Parker

Long-playing Records

It was the time when long-playing records were taking over from the old 78s. The first music we ever heard in Hatfield was when we visited a colleague of Frank's who lived in the middle block of flats in Roe Green Lane. He was quietly spoken, gentle and mild-mannered but he had a hi-fi record player, and amplifier and a huge speaker. The music was always turned up rather louder than I liked. His wife told me that once the people in the flat above had knocked on the floor when he was playing music late at night. He had leapt up and banged on the ceiling in retaliation. By the time we moved into 27 Bishops Rise in 1955 we also had long-playing records; Frank used to buy them more cheaply through a record club. It was so lovely to be able to play through long pieces of music without having to turn over the record every four and a half minutes as with 78s.

Janet Vann

CHAPTER 3

Working for de Havilland's and Others

The main administration building of the de Havilland Aircraft Company. (British Aerospace plc)

The subway for pedestrians and cyclists under the Barnet bypass from the aircraft company to St Albans Road, April 1965. (English Partnerships/Ken Wright)

Crossing the A1

I used to cycle to work, which took around 20 minutes. Crossing the A1 at 8.30 a.m. was very difficult. There were no underpasses and people wanting to cross used to collect in a great mass and then surge into the traffic – forcing it to stop for us. The same thing happened in the evening.

Clearing the Way

At de Havilland there was a hooter that went five minutes before closing time to allow for pedestrians and cyclists to get away. They were really strong on that. It was a five minute standstill for all cars.

Crowds and Crowds

I do remember the vast numbers of people coming to work and going from work, that's something that stays in my mind. People flocking to the gate and through the gate in a big surge.

Clocking On and Off

If you were at the end of the queue you might not have clocked out till 5.15; that wouldn't have made any difference but if you were three minutes late in the morning they stopped your money equal to fifteen minutes' work.

Frank Vann

34

The Firm's Time

If you were going out for a medical reason, or for some other reason leaving the site, you clocked off and then you handed your gate pass in at the police box. When you came in you clocked on again, and you were not paid for that time in the early days.

Jim Parker

Missile Mathematics

I worked at what was de Havilland Propellers on the first missile, codename Blue Jay. I was a mathematical assistant. We had to analyse the flight data, the telemetry as it was called. The instruments went up with the missiles and the data came down in different channels, and you had to analyse it and make graphs, and work out calculations on the adding machine. I saw the job advertised in the paper, I think; no qualifications were needed, you learnt as you went. It was just a small office. We had to have a pass with your photograph on to get in, and sign the Official Secrets Act. Once you were in you couldn't get out again without permission until it was time to go home.

Flying Records

In 1952 when John Cunningham was doing the first flights with the very first Comet, he was shooting off to all the usual capitals round Europe, setting up a new record. Within half an hour of

A Comet 1a used for infra-red testing. Barrie Smith, who was the flight engineer, is fourth from the left. (British Aerospace plc)

touch down, it had been radioed back, put on paper, and was on every notice board in the factory.

David Willson

Air Miles Fifties Style

After the Comet crashes, the Comet was re-designed and it was just at that time I joined de Havilland's in 1953. The original Comet was fitted with de Havilland engines, but the Comet II, which is the improved version, had Rolls Royce engines and to get a certificate of air worthiness for these engines they had to have done, I think, two thousand hours in flight. And so they fitted two Comet IIs with Rolls Royce engines and everyday they flew to Beirut and back. Those of us who had worked on the aeroplane were told we could fly to Beirut and have ten pounds for overnight expenses and fly back the next day. And lots of us did, we were just getting experience of the engine, we weren't testing it, just getting two thousand hours. There were four seats in the fuselage, the facilities were very primitive, it took about four or five hours to get there. We got off at Beirut and the next day when we went to get back, we heard that the aeroplane wasn't coming that day and we hadn't got enough money. There were no Barclaycards or anything and there were great currency restrictions, you couldn't get hold of money abroad. We were very worried for a time and then an aeroplane did eventually turn up to take us back to London.

Frank Vann

Jean Marshall in 1955, before she was involved in Meals on Wheels. (Jean Marshall)

The children's section of the de Havilland lending library on the opposite side of the Barnet bypass, next to Waters Garage. (British Aerospace plc)

The World's First Jet Airliner

The company allowed employees to experience the novelty of jet travel by allocating seats on many proving flights. These were quite random, it might be a short check flight occupying one of the few seats in a sparsely furnished machines or a much longer route simulation in a fully furnished aircraft with catering etc. My flight was in an afternoon on one of the former, whilst the airline pilots were trained. The booking procedure from the Propeller side was to ring John Cunningham's PA and ask to be put on the list, then wait for the call.

Food Quality

There was an enormous bust-up over the quality of the food, I remember.
There were always strikes threatened and the like. So there was an Aircraft Group Canteen Committee formed and it took over everything to do with the food.

Jim Parker and another

Overalls, Dresses and Seats

At the Propeller Site it was a one-level canteen and people went in there in their overalls. Office workers and young women in their dresses went in and sat on the same chairs; there were complaints about the dirt from some of them.

Meals on Wheels

The nearest I ever got to de Havilland's was that I did Meals-on-Wheels and I remember being taken round to the back of the canteen to collect the meals. They were preparing two or three thousand meals a day, anyway.

Jean Marshall

Bread and Dripping

I remember the canteen for bread and dripping, because we used to occasionally work on a Saturday morning and it was actually a treat. People were still eating bread and dripping and it was a highlight to go into the canteen on a Saturday morning and have it.

Shirley Knapp

Cutlery Washing

I remember the restaurant when I was working there on my holiday work, there was something funny about cleaning the cutlery. You had to wash your own cutlery in a great big tank, or something.

Pat Lewis

Cutlery Care

You could buy your cutlery. I've still got mine I think.... You took it back to your own department and washed it.

Barrie Smith

Guests for Lunch

I think the main canteen was open seven days a week, and they also used to do for people living on their own, they could walk in and go into the canteen. Retired and living on their own, instead of having meals on wheels, or going down to a lunch club, they went into the canteen. I suppose they were well known to the policeman on the gate who watched where they went.

David Willson

Overtime Pay

On monthly-paid staff it wasn't until my last three years that I got paid for over-time – and you did a lot of it.

Barrie Smith

Hours of Work

I worked from eight until five-thirty when I first started at Hatfield. You had to work forty-four hours in 1950, cut down to forty-two then to forty, thirty-nine and then thirty-seven.

David Willson

Managing the Unpaid Month

When I was promoted, we went from weekly pay to monthly pay, so that was another stretch. It was also being paid into the bank and so the pay packets started disappearing. They told us it would take three months [to adjust]

An aerial view of the airfield, which also shows Lemsford Road and 'The Courts' flats in the foreground. (British Aerospace plc)

and it really did take three months. Don't forget nowadays there is always some money somewhere, either on a card, you can borrow, have an account, – but when we were first married we came back with our fare to work the next day, your wage lasted you the week. Having just moved into the house, there wasn't really any savings behind us at all, because we'd spent out to move. It was always a great financial strain when you changed from being weekly to monthly paid. After being paid every week you suddenly found, four weeks with no money. You were paid in arrears of course, so you had a blank month anyway. It was three months before you were able to manage. Thursday was quite a highlight. Thursday was pay-day.

Hours of work were long when there was engine running to be done, but it was always a very good life.

Barrie Smith

Apprentice School Reputation

The de Havilland's Apprentice School at Astwick Manor had a high reputation. It was important for the development of the company for the future. In August 1955 there were about 2,500 apprentices.

Frank Vann

Chris Church of Wellfield Road, Olympic cyclist and Puffin pilot, about to leave for the Tokyo Olympics in September 1964. (Ken Wright)

Worldwide Influence

One of the strongest organizations of the old people is the Technical Students' Association which is a very close-knit one. If you go around the world talking to heads of airlines, it's amazing how many of them started out in the de Havilland's Technical School. It was thought to be the place of excellence in training for aircraft design.

Frank Vann

De Havilland Propellers

A very successful sports and social club had been running in the Aircraft Company since 1935 and ten years later it had some 4,000 members in twenty-seven sections, including a works band. By 1950 it was felt that enough people were employed by de Havilland Propellers on the north side of the airfield to warrant their own club. An inaugural meeting was held on April 4 at which the Company undertook to provide a sports ground with clubhouse and equipment for cricket, soccer and rugby. Drama, bridge, athletics, social and golf sections soon followed. The initial membership was 334. On two evenings in January 1951 the drama group produced its first play, Somerset Maugham's The Breadwinner at Hatfield Public Hall. In 1960 the monthly subscription, deducted from wages, was one shilling.

Jim Parker

The Puffin Man-powered Aircraft

In the late Fifties and early Sixties, a group of enthusiasts from de Havilland decided to enter the competition for the Kramer Prize, which was to be given for the first man-powered aircraft to fly a mile in a figure of eight, at least 10ft off the ground. The leader and chief designer of the group was John Wimpenny. For a time he was also the chief pedaller. Frank was a structural expert helping with the design. The aircraft had to be very light and the balsa wood structure was covered in melamine, and when it flew it looked like a huge dragonfly and quite beautiful. It was very fragile and so only could be flown on a still dry morning or evening, out of factory hours. There was a team of people involved in the building and other people willing to help, and when the weather was right people would phone round.

I remember us getting a phone call one morning about 5.30 a.m. or 6 o'clock and Frank, Roderick and I cycled down to the factory to help wheel the 'Puffin' out of the hangar. It was a very delicate operation, and it took about half an hour to get it out on to the airfield. Eventually it flew $\frac{3}{4}$ mile – a record which stood for over ten years – and there was a great celebratory party. One of the pilots was Chris Church, the Hatfield Olympic cyclist.

Janet Vann

Benefits Passed On

There were buying afternoons on a Tuesday. You paid a handling charge but you got it very cheap. I remember buying car components, valves, car filters and bearings, but the stores had all kinds of things. If you bought mechanical parts they were a better standard than you would get through your garage, for a third of the price. So that was useful and anyone could do that.

Loss of Benefit

Anyone working with chemicals had a pint a day of milk extra because that counteracted the toxicity. Except

Miss de Havilland 1962. The winner is Denise Clark of the sales department (centre), second is Deborah Sugrue (left) and third Ruth Manning (right). (*Welwyn and Hatfield Times*)

in de Havilland's they got caught taking it home and it got stopped.

David Willson

Social Concerns

We had at one time thirty-six trades unions in that factory, covering that whole vast spectrum of activities, all fighting strongly for the rights of their workers. Locally another organization I was involved in, the Trades Council, was the local TUC, which brought together the trades unions acting in accord with one another on matters outside the factory, all local conditions, the housing, the health, the food, and a whole host of other things.

Frank Clayton

Providing for Future Workers

The AEU were very active, not so much on the staff side, but the works side certainly. Millie MacFee was a convenor, she worked on the shop floor at some time. 'Red Millie' as she was called spent her days up at Westminster lobbying to get the 146 built here. Very proud of that, she worked very hard.

Frank Clayton

Union Agreement

It was agreed that those who had come in during the war were in fact called 'dilutees'. The union allowed them on that basis: they would be the first to go.

Of course a lot of them, mainly women, became very good at their jobs and there was great pressure for some of them to be kept on in their jobs. But there were these written agreements by the AEU. They had to go and time-served men would then get their jobs back, and become the core of the post-war industry.

David Willson

First-class Care

There were excellent medical facilities at de Havilland's. I remember there were two or three nurses, Nurse Donaldson, Nurse Driver, Nurse Hagg and Nurse Sheldon, at different times. It was a real medical block, you almost felt they could do operations there. I don't think they actually did, but it was very good, and superbly equipped, and with a doctor, Dr Bishop.

David Willson

Health Check

I attended the Mass Radiography Chest X-ray unit at de Havilland's, Hatfield, in August 1948.

Reg Coleman

Prevention Better than Cure

Chest X-rays were well established by 1951. They had started in mining areas much earlier.

David Willson

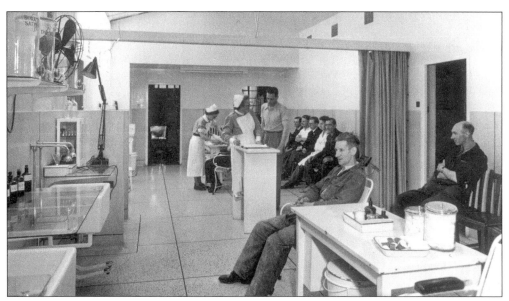

A medical room at de Havilland's. (British Aerospace plc)

Blood Donor Sessions

Once a month there were blood donor sessions. They obviously didn't catch the same people each month, but it was there. If you weren't well, (they always tested if you were a bit below par), they'd say, 'Go and see your doctor and get some iron pills, and come back in four weeks time.'

Passing Out

It was the men that used to pass out, they used to go down like flies, never the women.

No Running!

You had a restful afternoon when you gave blood, because you had to rest for so long afterwards. I remember I said, 'Hurry up, I've got to catch a bus,' and they said, 'Well you mustn't run for the bus!'

Jean Marshall

Emergency Blood Donors

The Harrow and Wealdstone train crash was on 8 October 1952. 112 people were killed and many more injured. A call went out right round the works for blood donors, and over 300 people presented themselves, gave about a pint each and if it had been possible to take it, they would have given twice as much. It was a double-headed train crash in the early morning fog. The fact that there were about 8,000 people here made it an obvious site to come to.

Of course when you weren't paid for sick leave you went back long before you should have done very often.

David Willson, Jim Parker and others

Sick Leave

It took years to get holiday and sick pay for the manual workers. You could start a secretary on at sixteen and she would get sick pay and a paid holiday. You could have a man in the shop, been there for twenty years, top man, your key man, he didn't get any sick pay, he didn't even get pay for a morning he might have to go and have an X-ray. Slowly it did get changed, but I always felt this was tragic.

Jim Parker

CND Effect

My husband worked for a local electrical firm, May & Roberts, and they contracted into de Havilland's. I remember we were members of CND at one time and there were some problems about the Official Secrets Act. He wouldn't sign it or something, but it was a handicap to working in there on a sub-contract basis.

Daphne Westwood

Short-lived Sickness

Of course, when you weren't paid for sick leave, you went back long before you should have done, very often.

Barrie Smith

The main administration building of Jack Oldings in 1952. The Tesco supermarket now stands on the site. (Ken Wright)

The Hatfield Laundry (Wellfield Road) annual dinner in the Memorial Hall, 1950. (Buxton-Smith)

Cook's Cases

Cooks Corrugated Cases was an important firm locally, which closed down in March in 1998. In 1963 Workers' Playtime visited to entertain 300 employees, with Charlie Chester and Ruby Murray top of the bill.

Ron Kingdon

Head Office at Hatfield

Lone-star Die Casting Tools Ltd made toy soldiers in metal and plastic, and also accurate die-cast metal components for outside firms, between 1953 and 1970. They had three overseas factories in 1968, as well as a head office and factory in Hatfield with others at Palmers Green and Welham Green.

Ron Kingdon

Setting up a Pharmacy

I knew the shop fitters on the Essex job quite well, and I approached them quite openly; if they did the job at Hilltop, they would have to give me credit, and take the cash over a period of time. In the same way I approached all the suppliers that I needed, all the wholesalers, and put the cards on the table. I went to see them in person and told them I'd do my best to pay as quickly as it was possible to do, but that there would be a delay of a couple of months before I could start making payments and so on. No one turned me down, you see things were different then. Commerce was different. It's hard now, people are not able to trust the word of others. People are not able to take the risk. But then, of course, things really were different.

Donald Hodson

CHAPTER 4
Shops, Shopping and Services

The Old Brewery Yard at the rear of Dollimore's shop on Brewery Hill in March 1967. From left to right: Vic Cull (Development Corporation), Lawrence Dollimore, John Challif of Manor Fruit Stores (now Hatfield DIY), Lionel Dollimore, Fred Harris (Development Corporation). (English Partnerships/Ken Wright)

Hatfield Market in 1967, showing David Dunkley's favourite wood stall. (English Partnerships/Ken Wright)

Market Trio

You see we didn't have the market to begin with. There wasn't a market, but then when the market came and we had these three men, Len, Ben and Aaron, with their material stalls we didn't have to go to St Albans so much.

Janet Vann

Market Off-cuts

There used to be a delightful guy on the market who sold wood off-cuts which was great because you could buy all sorts of bits from him – not huge bits like you can only get now. It was quite handy if you were trying to make something up. You'd go and buy a few off-cuts from him and he'd probably do what you wanted.

David Dunkley

Market Greetings

The greengrocers on the market were run by the same family, George and Rose. We used to have my brother's two little girls at weekends very often, as they were around the same age as my son and they loved coming down to the market because everyone said 'Good morning' to me and they thought I was ever so famous!

June Smith

White Lion Square in 1965, with mothers and children, prams and tricycles outside Woolworth's. (English Partnerships/Ken Wright)

Quick Shift

Quite often I bought material in the market. Buy the material Saturday morning, go to work in it on Monday because they were so simple, just shift dresses in those days.

Talking about Tingey's

We bought our larger perambulator at Tingey's, a Marmet. In those days you'd see large displays of these prams, big things, not those collapsible buggy-type things, you had a coach!

You could buy toys at Tingey's.

There was Tingey's Corner, a little hardware shop where you could buy virtually anything. Alf Walters was the man in there, a very good shop.

The great thing was before all these bubble-packs, if you wanted two screws you just bought two screws. Tingey's had all those lovely drawers and little boxes full of different bits.

I used to come out from the Company to get components from Tingey's. Whatever I've wanted they have found for me up there.

There were two biggish furniture places in Hatfield. One was Tingey's, later Whites of Cheltenham (where Pizza Hut is now) and the Co-op had a big furniture side; you could furnish a house quite easily from Hatfield shops.

When the grocers at Tingey's changed into a supermarket, I remember a friend saying, 'I'm so worried that I'll put things into the basket and walk out.'

Jim Parker, Janet Vann and others

School Uniform Buying

Richardson's, on the Parade near the old Bus Garage, sold school uniforms, but you couldn't get Howe Dell there; you had to go to St Albans.

Claire Figg

Uniform Shoes

Towards the end of the 1960s we had the cost of school uniforms and also of shoes. We had to go to Victor Modes in St Albans for the school uniforms, but the shoes were bought near the bus garage here. My only way round it was to select two or three pairs and let the children choose out of those. When Hatfield School first started they stated the style of shoe and that was a great help to all us mums. I can remember school uniform being quite a thing as having got three children it was a big outlay. Some schools helped if necessary, but it was kept very private between the parents and the school.

June Smith

Pharmacies and Other Shops

There was a sense of idealism around, and I think the Development Corporation felt that they ought to be encouraging the young businessman. I had only just recently opened exactly the same sort of shop on a newly built estate at Aveley in Essex, admittedly only as a manager, but satisfactorily. I'd

The Hilltop shops in 1963 – note the large prams and old-style pushchairs, not a buggy anywhere. (English Partnerships/Ken Wright)

49

done exactly what it was they were looking for someone to do. Anyway to cut it short, I got the shop [at Hilltop] .We actually opened in Easter week 1957 in one of the Wimpey houses in Hawthorns, as a temporary shop. I was very fortunate because in the following winter there was quite a serious flu epidemic, and that helped to set me on the road. The number of prescriptions was very large for a shop like that. I was able to pay off the bills reasonably quickly.

Donald Hodson

Nina Barnes

When we moved to Roe Green in March 1955 there weren't any shops there then, but they built them before the end of the year. We had Nina Barnes the chemist; that was wonderful; if she didn't have something in she would get it by the next day. She weighed the babies, nothing was too much trouble.

Janet Vann

A Good Range of Shops

You could clothe your children at Hilltop. There was an outfitters, men's clothes, schoolchildren's clothes and so on. I believe it was called Green's.

Shirley Knapp

Twin Pram

Jennings was the Hilltop toy shop and they sold prams as well. When we had

Donald Hodson's temporary chemists shop at 11 The Hawthorns in 1957. (Donald Hodson)

our first twins, they imported one from Denmark especially for us, a twin pram where the babies lay side by side because I didn't want head to foot. That part lifted out like a carrycot so that you could take it in the car. That was in 1962, but to start, the twins were in a single pram, they used to suck each other's thumbs.

Ann Dunkley

Tin Money and Club Books

We had no shops in South Hatfield; Oxlease was still countryside. I walked with Christine down to Hatfield to Williams Bros near the Curzon Cinema. They gave tin tokens with your change, which could be cashed back at 1/- for £1 worth of tin tokens. South Hatfield shops were built at the same time as St John's church; the big shop nearest Bishops Rise was the Co-op, Fine Fare had the other end one. We had our own post office instead of going to Roe Green, a butcher, greengrocer; Keco sold most DIY and hardware; Young's had a small shop for electrical goods. We also had a wool shop, a chemist and the rent office. Most people had a Club Book as there were very few clothes and linen shops in Hatfield. With young children it was not easy to go on buses to St Albans, although we did at sale times.

Jessie Axford

Bill Webster, the keenest supporter of Hatfield Town FC and brother of Webster the butcher in St Albans Road. (*Welwyn and Hatfield Times*/Denis J. Williams)

Shopping Choice

I know at another time we used to use the local shops at Hilltop, which were here when we arrived. The church wasn't, but the shops were, and we used Fine Fare for the groceries and Young's for our electrical requirements, Keco's for hardware, and Green's for the children's clothes as they grew up. We could get most things that we required there, and of course with the pram it was an extremely useful shopping centre, because it was in easy walking distance, but we did also use the town centre. We bought furniture from Tingey's, and larger ironmongery from

51

A view of the town centre in 1968, showing the Gracemead Cottages at the rear of the Market Place, which were demolished to make way for the Woolco development. (English Partnerships/Ken Wright)

Tingey's, and went down to Sheriff's for our horticultural requirements. I bought clothes in the old town, at Drury's and at Hankin's, we certainly did use it. Whilst my wife was working I used to use Taylor's for tobacco requirements, and boxes of chocolates which were always neatly wrapped. He insisted on wrapping everything before you left the shop, no matter how many people were waiting behind.

Gerald Model

Off-licences

There were no supermarkets selling drink then, just the off-licence. There were three off-licences in Hatfield in 1966. There was Norman's by the bus garage, a Victoria Wine store in the shop nearest the swimming pool and Arthur Cooper down the bottom of Crawford Road, but it was mostly bottled beer that they sold.

Casual Style

Randalls sold the camping equipment on one side, and in another shop next door, at the corner of the market place, it had perhaps not suits, but sports jackets and slacks; as a men's outfitters, it offered a very good service.

Jean Marshall

Bargain Hunter

I would cycle down to Hatfield to get something that was 'thruppence a pound' cheaper than the mobile shops that came around. If there was a bargain going somewhere, I heard about it and would go on the bike to get it.

Changing Scenery

In 1968 the Hatfield Rural District Council gave their support for a large multiple store in the town centre known as Woolco. The £1.5 million scheme with its many self-service units would require forty-eight cottages and sixty-six garages in the Queensway car park to be demolished. Most of the residents of the cottages had already been re-housed.

Ron Kingdon

Matching Beads to Shoes

I remember going to Johns' shoe shop when we had the foundation stone laid for St John's church. I wanted red shoes and red beads and I went into Johns' and decided on a pair of shoes, but wasn't quite sure of the colour, because I'd seen some red beads in a little shop in the Old Town. So I took one shoe and went and bought my beads to match the shoe.

June Smith

Cine Camera Shop

I was given a cine camera for my birthday in 1959, so I became interested in Stewart Cameras which was in the town centre at that time. The other place where we used to buy cine equipment and film and so on was

June and Barrie Smith at the reception held at the Technical College after the St John's Foundation Stone Ceremony in June 1958. June is wearing her matching shoes and beads. (Barrie Smith)

Sydney Rumbelow's shops on the corner of Park Street in Old Hatfield. (English Partnerships/Ken Wright)

Boots in Hatfield, it was very good. There was also a chap at Ekins and Fisher who was a great enthusiast.

David Dunkley

Chiropody Practice

In those days the professions were very strict about advertising and you were only allowed to put four advertisements into a local paper, announcing the setting up of a practice. I then did some fairly unprofessional things, introducing myself personally to people who were in business, and almost anyone else who I could introduce myself to, in the hope that they may know someone who required my services.

Gerald Model

Cricketer's Return

In 1964 Freddie Titmus, the Middlesex and England test cricketer, bought 'Toms', the newsagent's and tobacconist's shop in Manor Parade, Hatfield Garden Village. He was coming to live in Hatfield when he returned from India where he was touring with the MCC. His wife's parents had already moved into the shop, the first one he had bought. 1963 was his benefit year and his off-spin bowling had been a great success in Australia.

Ron Kingdon

Sydney Rumbelow

My memories of Sydney Rumbelow are of going into his shop in Old

54

Hatfield on a Saturday afternoon to buy a record. The shop would be empty, the door bell rang, we waited and Sid came from the back room where he had been working on a radio or a television set. He served us and had a chat, the phone rang, very often, and it would be a call for him to go and sort out a television set. As we went out of the shop he would follow us out. Most days he was working on his own, he locked up, got in his van and went off. On other occasions, close to six o'clock, (in those days it was regulated closing time), he would follow us out of the door, lock up and rush off home. He had his own small dance band and would be on the stage, either at the Cranborne Rooms at the Red Lion, at the Old Public Hall, the Memorial Hall (opposite St Luke's church), the Community Centre in Welwyn Garden City or even the Market Hall in St Albans. Sid didn't waste much time; he was on the stage every evening, seven days a week, as well as working in his shop from 8.30 a.m. to 6.00 p.m.

David Willson

Necessary Low Profile

You always used to have to be careful when you went in the hairdressers, Mr and Mrs Tasho, because you weren't supposed to go during works time. As you got on a bit you thought you could risk it and you'd find yourself sitting in the next chair to one of the directors, and keeping a very low profile.

Frank Vann

Hairdresser Moments

I went to Tasho's and he used to shut on Saturday lunchtime. They weren't open in the afternoon and I've got very thick hair and he was quite sure, yes, we can get your perm done by lunchtime. I said that it wouldn't dry and he said 'Yes, yes. We've got a new machine.' About three o'clock we got away!

Janet Vann

A seasonal advertisement from Sydney Rumbelow.

Shops on Brewery Hill, Old Hatfield, in March 1967. (English Partnerships/Ken Wright)

Little and Often

My daughter-in-law said to my wife not long ago, 'How did you manage when you had a young family and you hadn't got a car to go shopping?'. She said that we had no problems – we went shopping three or four times a week. There were no such things as multi-packs of toilet rolls and things like that, it was all small packs, so we just bought enough. People had not got fridges and things like that. We had our wheeled baskets and went and did our shopping.

Barrie Smith

Home Service

I certainly know that our groceries at one time were bought from Carver's, down in the parade in St Albans Road, Hatfield, now St Albans Road East. He used to come up one day to take an order and deliver it the next. Our meat came by the mobile butchers, Butlers, who used to come along and stop outside the house. He more or less knew the sort of things that we would want and had a supply of those things. He came two or three times a week, and once a week we would normally have Carver's.

Gerald Model

Home-made Cakes Service

In the Ellenbrook Lane area someone came round almost every day. We met our neighbours through that. Tingey's came and it wasn't any more expensive than it was if you went down there. Tingey's twice a week; greengrocers twice a week (different ones); a home-made cake lady. When things were rationed, and there were no eggs, we welcomed her with open arms.

Peggy Jones

Twice-weekly Shops on Wheels

We didn't go shopping; we had Mr Bradley in his bus come round the area twice a week in 1953 and 1954, and he brought everything. We bought our bread and our vegetables from him. My baby was due in 1954 and we were living in Days Mead and every week I had my peanuts and peaches, which was my fad at that time.

June Smith

I Never Went Shopping

In those days everything was delivered. I never did any shopping as I have to do now. Tingey's delivered the groceries, Dollimore's delivered the greengroceries, the baker came, and the laundry came round, and the milkman.

Talking about Mobile Shops

When I first came to Hatfield in '53, it was just a few houses and lots of mud, and these people who came delivering were so welcome.

We got to know our neighbours through waiting for the vans.

We had two grocery men who came round, and a fish man and a potato man.

The Co-op always came round with the milk, and they always had provisions.

The milk came round with a horse and cart. They used to stop next door but one, but if I was able I was always the first one to go and get a pail and shovel!

Jim Parker Jessie Axford, and others

CHAPTER 5

Family Life and Children's Health

Her Majesty the Queen speaks to Mrs Margaret Nicholas of Cecil Crescent during the royal opening of the QE2 Hospital. (*Welwyn and Hatfield Times*/ Denis J. Williams)

Tingey's shop in St Albans Road, on the corner of Dog Kennel Lane. Boots the Chemist now stands on the site. (English Partnerships/Ken Wright)

Family Accounts

In November in one week in 1969 I had spent £1 6s 1d on greens, £3 17s 8d at the grocers, £2 11s 7d on meat and fish, 1s 10d on bacon, 11s 2d for milk, 2s 10d at the chemist, £1 2s 5d for household things. Then I'd spent £3 6s 11d on myself. As this was the end of November, I was probably buying Christmas gifts.

I remember in the late '50s having £3 for my whole week's shopping, and that included the joint for the weekend, all my meat and greengrocery and everything else.

Janet Vann

Family Meals

I went home for a cooked lunch every day and my wife had two children to look after. You know it was fantastic. You ask a young wife today to operate that kind of arrangement!

Once or twice we had to have our main meal in the evening. My husband then realised how nice it was to have a leisurely meal and to be able to sit around the table with the children and talk instead of having to rush the meal in that hour and rush home from work and back. So from then on it was always a snack lunch and a meal in the evenings. When it came to weekends, even Sundays, we still did it because it allowed us to go out for the whole day and enjoy the day together.

Although they'd had a main meal at midday, we always had what we called a 'knife and fork tea' and we all had it together.

Jim Parker and others

Dinner was Dinner Time

Dinner was dinner time. Everybody came home at dinner time, the children all came home from school and Frank used to walk home from work, from de Havilland's because the dinner hour was long enough.

They Never Helped Themselves

I used to be rotten to my kids. I would never cook anything after teatime evening meal. If they wanted anything else they did it themselves. I taught them to make toast and they did beans on toast. Then we went through a session of pancakes but they had to do it themselves. I always knew exactly what had gone out of the fridge and what had gone out of the cupboard. Now children help themselves! It is probably because the women are working and they are not there, but I don't think mine ever helped themselves.

Our TV was never allowed on at meal times. We always sat down and had ours in the dining room.

June Smith and Claire Figg

Camp Coffee

I did have ordinary coffee but I had to have Camp Coffee when my mother-in-law came, that's all she drank.

Puddings

For puddings we had custard, semolina, junket, jellies, milk jellies, apple fritters, milk puddings with fresh milk, evaporated milk, jellies with Carnation cream, mousses, spotted dick, jam roly-poly.

The English Ate Meat Every Day

I had a penfriend and I went on holiday to Holland in 1962/63 to stay with her. The first thing she asked me was whether it was true that English people ate meat everyday. And it was true and she was amazed.

R in the Month for Pork

Pork we didn't have unless there was an R in the month. Sprouts and parsnips you didn't have until they were frosted. And we didn't have any grapes.

Never Heard of Chicken Kiev

The meal was always served at half past five or six. We'd never heard of Chicken Kiev or exotic foods that we eat these days, and we don't have the seasonal things. I miss that. When the new potatoes came in they weren't Egyptian, they were English new potatoes from Jersey.

Shirley Knapp

Home from School

Ours, they would have a cup of tea, it was always ready for them when they came in from school. We were great tea drinkers, and they were allowed one plain biscuit and one cream biscuit. My daughter is now forty-six, and still she will never pick out two cream biscuits. But cakes were for tea, they weren't for when you first came in from school – we always had a tin full of cakes.

June Smith

Five Butchers!

I was sharply aware of the fact that there were five butchers in the town centre here. You could go and choose. I could spend all Tuesday choosing my joints and things.

David Cregan

Post-war Rationing

All rationing only finally finished on 4 July 1954. Each week I used to get 2oz of sweets, 2oz of butter, 4oz of marge, 2oz of tea, 4oz of sugar and one egg a week. It was adequate and balanced.

If you had chickens I think you got special meal instead of your egg ration, and there were a lot of people around here who grew their own vegetables and fruit.

If you had a green ration book, which was for an unborn child, you were entitled to bananas, but you still had to queue and only if they were in the shop. If the word went round there were bananas you went and queued and hoped.

A boys' cookery class at the Breaks Youth Club in around 1953. (*The Hertfordshire Mercury*)

Bread Rationing

Bread wasn't rationed during the war but of course it was after the war. We were on holiday in Skegness and we were starving hungry and bread rationing had come in. We sent an SOS to our neighbours, 'Please send us some bread coupons, because we can't buy a bun in a shop or anything'. We were starving!

Nelly the Elephant

I remember Bishops Rise children used to come round and play records on Saturday morning when they were junior school age – records such as 'Nelly the Elephant', a selection from Snow White, etc. They had biscuit and squash for refreshment.

Janet Vann

Hatfield School Swimming Pool

Hatfield School had a swimming pool. You had to go with your children because there were no swimming guards on duty. The parents built that, they raised the money and built it, the PTA.. During the late Fifties, lots and lots of families went there everyday because you didn't have to pay, because you were part of the PTA and because you had to be there you got friendly with each other.

June Smith

We Went to Bed Earlier Then

The children went to bed probably earlier than they do now. It ranged from the little ones about half past six onwards, to half past eight. We all went to bed earlier then. I think we'd probably be in bed by eleven.

June Smith

The Breaks Youth Club keep-fit group in 1951. (*The Herts Advertiser*)

A Bit Like Village Life

We were all young wives at home with children and it was a bit like village life. Everybody knew everybody in the particular area you were in and all the children played together and it was very nice. Everybody was very friendly and in the area we lived in, most people were the same sort of people, they had the same sort of interests and of course the children all went to school together.

Janet Vann

Dear Stream Woods

Dear Stream Woods, I think it was the greatest piece of preservation ever. I used to love it when the kids in the summer had all those swings and terribly dangerous things, the sort of thing to play on that nowadays no one would allow, were absolutely marvellous and provided by the Council. When we first moved into Wood Close, I remember counting at night on a summer evening, there would be forty children playing outside in that cul-de-sac, it was sheer joy. I had a camping van I used to use as a study, and at night there would be six or seven kids sleeping in the camping van. That certainly doesn't happen now, people lock their doors. We had all the doors open at one time. It didn't matter whose kids it was, if you were feeding children, it didn't matter whose they were.

David Cregan

Families Shared

We were lucky to live in a close with about twenty-odd houses and it made life easier. We all seemed to have our small children at the same time. We shared taking other children to school, to ballet lessons, play group etc. We had great activities going on in the close. One young girl used to organize a sports afternoon every year. She was fantastic, she would cut off the traffic at the end of the close and because there's a green in the centre, the children used to use the road as the running track. There was a communal dinghy, which was shared by several families. We used to take it to Wyboston at the weekends. Families shared in that way and we got to know each other very well.

Shirley Knapp

Getting Married

I got married in 1961 in Welwyn Garden City and had my reception at my parents' home in Holliers Way. I married my second husband here at the Registry Office. We didn't have a honeymoon, there wasn't money for that in those days. It was quite common not to have a honeymoon, money had to be watched very carefully. I can remember when I got married, my husband at the time was earning £9 1s a week.

Lyn Pedersen (née Vincent)

My wedding was in 1951 and we've still got the account. At the bottom was six bottles of wine to have with the cake at the end.

Barrie Smith

Wedding Cakes

If you had a three-tier wedding cake during food rationing you had your bottom layer made with cake mixture and then the top two were of wood.

In 1951 when I was married, you took your ingredients to the baker and all the ingredients went in together. They made the cake, but they weren't iced or anything, they were in a cardboard cover. You didn't get back from them as good ingredients as you gave, because they were mixed together with other people's ingredients.

Children's Health

A remarkable thing about living with the children as they were growing up, was that their health was attended to by a whole battery of possible surgeries, all of them purpose-built, not as in Manchester, run in the back of old garages with paraffin heaters and so on. Here you went to new buildings and you may have had to sit in the usual sort of queues, but at least it was comfortable.

David Cregan

Peartree Maternity Home

I went into Peartree Maternity Home and had Andrew on June 1st 1963, and they said we'd all got to transfer to

A Coronation street party in Birchwood Close, 1953. (Reg Coleman)

64

The Hilltop mother and baby clinic in 1965. (English Partnerships/Ken Wright)

QEII Hospital on the 10th, and I thought, 'Goodness, they're not going to send me there for one day?', because they usually sent you out on the tenth day. Then there was some hold-up, and they said they were not going to open until the autumn of 1963.

Janet Vann

The Baby Clinic

The baby clinic was held Friday afternoons, in the St John Mission Hall in College Lane; Nellie Dixon helped. The Hilltop pub (and community centre) opened in autumn 1959 and then a mother and baby club was started by the WRVS. In the summer of 1960 Roe Hill House was used instead, and I joined the WRVS to make it possible to run it. We found mothers and children under five enjoyed this Tuesday afternoon break together. It was not good in the winter months because of the distance, and meeting children from school, so the venue was changed to Downs Farm, where a lovely sized hall had been built. It was a very successful club, with old Mrs O'Brien, and then Mrs Jessie Jones, making the tea and orange squash, and washing up. We had a varied programme, and at Christmas we had a party and a present for all the children. I had thirty children under five to buy for, at a cost of 3s 6d each present. In the summer, through the WRVS, a coach was hired during the summer holiday, so school children went too, Wicksteed Park being a favourite place.

Jessie Axford

Toddlers on the way to the nursery at Roe Hill House in November 1960. Mrs E.M. Hindless of Bishops Rise was the supervisor. (*Welwyn and Hatfield Times*/Denis J. Williams)

They Almost Pushed You

I think they expected you at the baby clinic, they almost pushed you to go, the hospital would say, 'You know you've got to go.' A lot of it was social, probably. I mean, I was new to the town and it was a way of making contact, you met people.

Jean Marshall

Uncertainty

After you'd had the baby a health visitor would come in and give you all the 'gen'. There were mothers who were very uncertain. If your baby was doing all the things it should do, then OK, but if they had babies that didn't seem to grow properly, or eat properly then there were lots of people who really needed that support, so the clinics were invaluable.

June Smith

Calling the Doctor

I think that's why we often called the doctor, because we hadn't got older people to say 'Oh its only…'.

One of our girls had asthma very badly when she was small, and we had to have medication, and because she found it so difficult to sleep, they changed her over to a different medication, with a little bit of phenobarbitone in it, and I remember the doctor telling me that it would help her to sleep.

Janet Vann and Shirley Knapp

Polio Injections

I remember taking my children for polio injections, when they started in 1957 down in some huts near the Court House.

It all happened very suddenly. I went to Dr. Jones' surgery and we all had to go with our babies at once and then we had to go again three weeks later or something. Then later the cube of sugar came in. My two girls had the injections and every time they had one I had one mentally, but my youngest, Boyd, had the cube of sugar.

Janet Vann and June Smith

Concerns about Radiation

The radiation level worried me as a parent. Whenever I used to read about that I used to fear for my children and their future; every test that was being carried out pushed these levels up. Apart from that, all our academics felt that this was affecting all the world, and we couldn't do anything about it.

They used to measure sizes of feet for shoes with pediscopes. They were in every shoe shop. There were similar concerns about chest x-rays

Jim Parker, Shirley Knapp, Frank Vann

Miss Muriel Sherriff of Roe Green Lane just after completing forty years' service in baby clinics in Hatfield. She is holding Lyn Pedersen's (*née* Vincent) daughter Joanne, aged eight months. Joanne is now a schools inspector in information technology. (*Welwyn and Hatfield Times*)

Good Business for the Chemist

From the point of view of the pharmacy business, Hilltop was an excellent place, because there were so many children. Of course, the two classes of the population who actually go to the doctor and get prescriptions are old people and children. From the age of about twelve or fifteen to the age of about fifty or fifty-five, you don't go to the doctor. But I had all these thousands, it seemed like thousands, of children, babies, infants – and I was doing far more business than would be expected, because of the population distortion – and we had a really good few years.

Donald Hodson

Wellfield Hospital

There was Part 3 Accommodation for people at Wellfield House who really needed care. They didn't need nursing care, they needed supervision and observation, but they were supposed to be able to walk, either with a frame or with a stick. One of the things that really impressed me was the fact that the residents could go into Wellfield and still be part of the community. There was the post office, there was the town, you know, everything at that time was all around them. They could sit in the gardens, the library wasn't far away; I think it was a unique situation. And if the building had been suitable to keep that sort of arrangement it would have been wonderful, because the Part 3

White Lion Square before it was pedestrianized. Wellfield Hospital can be seen centre right – it is clear how close it is to the shops. (English Partnerships/Ken Wright)

Dr Burvill-Holmes outside Eastcote, his home and surgery on Brewery Hill. He was still practising at this time, March 1967. (English Partnerships/Ken Wright)

people just could come and go as they liked ... sometimes that was a disadvantage. We had one lady who was fond of having a Guinness and she'd often go off, or she'd apply for a job as a nanny. I had to go one night to pick her up from the station, some people had rung me from Surrey and said, 'We've got a woman here who said she lives at this address'. I said that this address was a hospital, 'She had come for an interview for a nanny'. You had the most extraordinary stories. There was never a dull moment.

Margaret Tyler

CHAPTER 6
Sunday Choice

Hatfield House and the Old Palace from the air, with St Etheldreda's church in the foreground. (British Aerospace plc)

Sunday Baking

With three very small children I did find it difficult to make cakes sometimes during the week and I used to get up about 6.30 on a Sunday to bake a sponge or something which I don't think many would do now.

I suppose because so many people were having roasts or oven-cooked meals, you just slipped some cakes in on another shelf or something. It was automatic. I remember we had a big earthenware bowl – a lovely stir of that!

It was sensible to bake cakes while you had got the oven on cooking the Sunday dinner. I used to try and do everything at once and then the dinner was delayed.

Shirley Knapp, Jim Parker and Janet Vann

Sunday Tea

Sunday tea was always very special inasmuch as in the summer we had things like salads. There was usually jelly and perhaps some fruit and I loved making cakes and so we always had two or three. In the winter it was more the things they loved like beans or scrambled eggs on toast for Sunday tea. Invariably we were always there, we did go out visiting sometimes, but tea and dinner we always sat at the table. Everybody did, it was the normal practice. They were only allowed to have a plate on their knee if they were poorly; if they were wrapped up in a chair in a blanket, then they were all right.

Constance Schofield

'Paddy's Wigwam'

One of the things which happened very early in the Sixties was the building of the Catholic church up in Bishops Rise, which provided another set of community buildings with money that initially came from outside the town. Later in the decade they rebuilt Marychurch in Old Hatfield, very much in the style of the cathedral in Liverpool, which the irreverent referred to as 'Paddy's Wigwam', but it was a smart interesting building. The Anglican churches weren't left out either, because they built the one at St John's, again a modern building, a little bit like an upturned longship in some ways. You see it there from the main road; it's quite a landmark. Of course at the time it was built it was just about on the parish boundary between North Mymms and Hatfield. We tend to forget that in those days the parish boundary ran through somebody's front room in Willow Way, there were boundary oaks in Lane End, and it went down back to Peter's Café and across the other side and into Bullens Green.

Bill Storey

Shilling Bricks

The vicarage was built and Revd David Farmborough and his wife Angela lived there. Angela started a Women's Fellowship, we met in the hall of Hazelgrove School. Sunday worship was held in the Cavendish Hall and my son Michael was christened there in February 1959. We bought one shilling bricks each week, having cards marked in bricks, for the church building fund. We carried on

St Peter's Roman Catholic church on Bishops Rise in May 1964. (English Partnerships/Ken Wright)

with the shilling bricks for the youth club and community hall which were built.

Jessie Axford

Sunday School and Evening Service

I had to go to morning Sunday school, afternoon Sunday school and then the evening service. When you were promoted from Sunday school you went to Bible class. In the end I became a Sunday school superintendent for the morning Sunday school, until I went to college. Once a year you had a lovely new dress for the Sunday school anniversary, and you all stood there in your new dresses wearing flowers. We had Scripture examinations and we went over to Dagnall Street Baptist church, which is in St Albans, for the presentation of certificates and other events. There were not many people living in the area who actually went there. I think it was my mother's background which influenced us, as she was a staunch Methodist from 'up

North'. You didn't dare to say you weren't going, even as a teenager.

Pat Lewis

Evangelical Church

In 1966, the South Hatfield Evangelical Church was built and opened in The Wades, South Hatfield. This church started with a few Christians who used to meet in a room in the Toc H building (now the Post Office sorting office). When this closed in 1951, they continued to meet in the house of Olive and Bob Bushnell in Crawford Road, but moved to the Roe Green Mission Room as the Brethren Assembly when St John's transferred to Cavendish Hall. The church grew rapidly and eventually moved to The Wades in 1966.

Shirley Knapp

Evensong was the Thing

St Ethelreda's was the first place I was introduced to when I came here in 1954. The Communion Service took a lower order in things in those days. Evensong was the thing you all dressed up for because everybody was there. Everybody who was important in the town, from the Dollimores, the Tingeys, Mr Copus, who ran the bank in Old Hatfield, all those people were there in their finery, so you couldn't come in anything else really. It was very definitely a social gathering at that time.

Fundraising Football Pools

The Catholic Church Hall and Presbytery in Bishops Rise were completed in 1961 at a cost of £75.000. In order to establish a regular income for St Peter's church, parishioners were invited to a dinner, laid on by the parish priest, Fr J. Church Milne. We were all gathered up on buses and taken down to Onslow school for this dinner, and everybody was told that a new scheme was coming about. Parishioners had to say how much they were going to give, and this was the nucleus of the income. The football pools went on to become the 200 or 400 club, based on the number of members, and with this lump sum coming in regularly, the fund went on for many years. All the donations to the football pools helped to pay off the interest and the main debt on the church which stood at £40,000 in November 1964.

Valerie Turley

St John's church at Hilltop under construction in 1958. (Photo Art)

Sunday Clothes

The children always had Sunday clothes. When you went visiting they didn't go out in jeans and a sweater, they went dressed up. There was a change when people started wearing jeans. I used to go to the Methodist church when it was in Roe Hill House before it was in the hut and in the Morley's house. A lot of us used to wear best hats and I'd always been brought up to understand that you dressed up on a Sunday and you had your Sunday clothes. Even though we lived quite near Oxlease I used to be dashing down at the last minute and one of the men said to me, ' I think you come in late to make a sensation!' and I hadn't realized that most of the other women weren't dressed up in hats and coats. At about the same time our son was in St Etheldreda's choir, and we went once or twice to services and I was quite appalled to see him in desert boots and jeans. At the same time we went to visit my brother and his wife, and they were going to take a snap, a photograph of all the family and our son had gone in jeans. My sister-in law told him that he must change out of his jeans to be in the photograph. He refused so we didn't get the photograph done. I suppose that was 1960 and that's when there seemed to be a change.

Janet Vann

Covered Heads

I remember well into the Sixties people wore hats and gloves and children were dressed up to go to church. When entering a Catholic church, people will remember, most women covered their heads. It happens very rarely now. I think young people would stare if they saw women wearing black veils (mantillas) over their heads, but well into the Sixties that was the case.

Sunday Choices

I don't think everybody went to church on Sunday or wore their best clothes. I had to work long hours so I just had the Sunday more or less to myself. In 1955 we moved into a new house, so for me, along with our neighbours, Sunday was the day to do the garden, lay the paths, put the garage and sheds up. You just didn't have the time for church. Then you visited your mother and father back wherever they lived, took the kids for cycle rides and things like that.

We Always Went Out

When the children were quite little I was the one who encouraged them to go to Sunday School because it was something I'd always had to do and I thought my children must too. But as my children got older it dropped off and I realized that I couldn't and you shouldn't influence them. Then we started to take them horse-riding at Mill Green on Sunday mornings and then we'd probably go out as well later in the day. We always went out on Sundays, we always did something, we never stayed in.

Barbara Latham

Sunday was our day out when we used to go to Hemel Hempstead, Dunstable, Hatfield Park, St Albans to walk to play or just to go out rambling and picnicking.

Some Sundays we Had a Car

Some Sundays, as our two sons got older, we arranged to have a car, and we used to take them to Hartham Park in Hertford. We also used to take them fishing. We used to go swimming as a family, sometimes we would meet up with friends over at Hertford but most Sundays it was cooking, doing the lunch and making a special cake for afternoon tea. We used to do a lot of walking in Hatfield Park, or we might make a trip to St Albans and have a walk by the lakes or go a bit further and have a picnic somewhere. We would go to church in the morning and our children went to St Johns.

Joyce Chapman

Minnows and Sticklebacks

On warm Sunday afternoons, I would pack our tea into a basket on wheels, for our picnic on the heath. The children would wade in the stream, catching minnows and sticklebacks. We walked through bluebell woods; the field on the other side grew lovely mushrooms, and both raspberries and blackberries grew on the hillside.

Jessie Axford

Michael Marlow in 1961. He has been involved with St John's church since its consecration.

Visiting Relatives

Sunday was for visiting relatives, going back to North London either to a sister-in-law or my parents; both our parents lived nearby each other. We used to go on the bus, the Green Line; it used to be one and threepence to Whetstone and a shilling from Whetstone. We usually had a twenty-minute wait in between; very often it was raining and we were there with the family and Boyd was a baby. My mother would very often instruct my father to bring us back, but otherwise we'd come back late afternoon and have the evening at home.

June Smith

CHAPTER 7
Free Time

The Breaks Youth Club netball team in May 1962. They had represented the county for the previous five years. From left to right: Sandra Baker (captain), Marion Prescott, Pat Vyse, Sandra Stratton, Iris Barratt, Pamela Disdale, Madeleine Thomson. (*Welwyn and Hatfield Times*/Denis J. Williams)

The Breaks Youth Club choir in around 1953. (*The Hertfordshire Mercury*)

Young People and Teenagers

The wonderful thing about living in the centre of a new town was that there were youth clubs. They did a great job with my children from the age of about ten to the age of about thirteen but you became aware as the children were growing older that there was very little for them to do, except hang around in the town centre.

David Cregan

The Breaks

The very first meeting of what was to become the Hatfield Youth Centre was held at St Audrey's School hall one evening in late spring/early summer in 1951, advertised by a small notice on the school notice board. Little did I know how many wonderful people I would meet when our small group was transferred to The Breaks – Bill and Rose Salmon, Ron and Inga Menday, and the various people who took part in the many activities which we were lucky to have access to. Scottish dancing with Mrs Bird, Keep Fit, the choir, later to become Hertfordshire Girls' Choir, netball and rounders for the girls. The primary activity for the boys was, of course, football. Drama was the foremost joint activity and the highlight of the year was without a doubt the Christmas Pantomime, performed at various locations in Hatfield. How lucky we were to have as the two bases for our youth centre The Breaks and later the Fiddle Bridge building, which de Havilland's kindly allowed us to use. I well remember how envious other clubs were who came to visit us. I'm sure that we all appreciated it. I know that when the 'boys' went to do their National Service, one of the first places they went to while on leave was The Breaks.

Diana Turner (née Jennings)

The Lemsford Café

In 1958 the Lemsford Café decided to close on Sunday evenings and not open until midnight – most unusual hours, one might think. The reason given by the owner, Mrs G. Clark, was that it was for the benefit of her real customers, the long-distance lorry drivers. Previously the café was opened at 8pm and all through the night on Sundays but this attracted large numbers of teenagers who would spend the whole evening over a cup of coffee and occupying all the chairs. The attraction for them was that these premises were the only ones in the district to possess a jukebox.

Ron Kingdon

One Bell Public House

As a young teenager I used to go down to the One Bell Public House in Old Hatfield. My best friend lived at the One Bell which isn't there now. It was quite naughty really going through the bar, because my mother was

a staunch Methodist and I used to go through the bar up to my friend's room. As a hobby we used to write down the words to the songs on Radio Luxembourg. In my first book the first words that I wrote down were 'April in Paris'.

Pat Lewis

Mods and Rockers

The Sixties saw the emergence of the 'Mods and Rockers' scooter versus motorbike groups. Following disturbances at Whitsun at certain seaside resorts in 1964 Hatfield police were warned of coming trouble at The Breaks youth club and further along at the Hilltop. Although there was plenty of activity with the two-wheeled vehicles dashing around, the extra contingent of police brought in prevented all but a few minor clashes. In the same year it was reported that the police were investigating groups of teenagers owing to a sudden flood of the 'Purple Heart' pills into the Hatfield area. Certain lads were making trips to Soho to purchase the drug at around one shilling and sixpence each.

Ron Kingdon

Dancing and Music Bands

During the Sixties there were many successes in the entertainment business involving musicians from Hatfield. It is an impressive list considering the size of the town, all of whom have achieved considerable world wide success: The ones who I remember are:

Mick Taylor – John Mayall and The
  Rolling Stones
Brian Glascock – The Motels
John Glascock – Jethro Tull
Paul Griggs – Guys and Dolls
Nigel Griggs – Split Enz
Alan Shacklock – Babe Ruth
Colin Blunstone – The Zombies
Barbara Gaskin – solo
Donovan – solo

In 1963, my brother Paul formed The Cortinas, all band members from Hatfield; I was just fourteen. The band built up a big following locally, playing regularly at The Hilltop, Cavendish Hall, and The Breaks Youth Centre in Hatfield and The Hop in Welwyn Garden Cty. My mother was manager and my father roadie. Pop music, and the hysteria which surrounded it, was also prevalent, to a lesser degree, in local areas. There was a huge interest and competitiveness amongst the local fans. I was still at school and I remember girls following me home, stealing my football shorts and leaving lipstick messages all over the band van. It was never difficult filling up a couple of coaches with fans for a band contest in London. In 1967, we turned professional and changed our name to Octopus. We ventured further afield and built up a big following in the Nottingham and Sheffield area.

I played football with Mick Taylor at Gascoigne Primary, but he progressed musically to join John Mayall and later the Rolling Stones. The two Glascock brothers Brian and John were both highly respected musicians. For a while

Donovan, who achieved international fame as a song-writer and folk singer in the Sixties. He lived on Bishops Rise. (*Welwyn and Hatfield Times*)

Brian drummed with Octopus before departing for the USA where he later joined The Motels, while John went on to play bass with Jethro Tull.

Octopus broke up in 1972 and the various member scattered. My brother, Paul found success with Guys and Dolls, while in 1977, I joined the legendary New Zealand band, Split Enz, and spent nearly eight years with them until the break up in 1984.

Bill and Rose Salmon and The Breaks Youth Club really provided a focus for young people and their various projects and ideas. For me it provided a social environment I had never experienced before. For The Cortinas, in those early days, The Breaks was our home – we rehearsed there for years, performed there and indeed spent most of our time there.

Nigel Griggs

Donovan

It was not unusual in the early Sixties to see Donovan, as a teenager, in the days before he became famous, sitting on the grass verge at the junction between Heron Way and Woods Avenue, playing his guitar.

Valerie Turley

Other Local Bands

There was Billy Hill and the Bluebirds and Sid Rumbelow. Sid was one of the main people. He had a big band group of about ten. There was another group who used to play here called Turners Group who came from Watford. There was a chap named Dillon who used to come from Welham Green. He used to play up there quite a lot and he used to play in Billy Hills Band quite a lot as well. He was a saxophonist. And they had a lad called Louis Badham. He was a brilliant pianist, and he used to play for all of these bands that went to these public halls.

Since 1958 there were weekly jazz concerts at the Red Lion.

It was the Cranborne Rooms I remember going to. There was Acker Bilk, George Melly, Chris Barber.

It was local bands that use to play at ballroom dances but it was London-based jazz bands that came out to these weekly sessions.

Frank Vann, Ken Wright, Shirley Knapp

A Scout Troop of Seventy-two

I was deeply involved in the Scouts in Muswell Hill and when I moved out here I thought it a good time for a rest and didn't do anything for a year. The third Hatfield Scout group met up on the corner opposite where Aldykes goes round onto Cavendish Way and I said to my wife, 'I miss the Scouts, I'll go back and see what I can do.' I went back and said, 'I'll be a Rover and then an Instructor.' That was 1953 and I'm still there! I've had most grades other than District Commissioner. It gave us a good basis for friends in Hatfield. In Muswell Hill, we used to like to keep a troop of twenty-four scouts, and you had a job to keep all the patrols up to six each. When I got out here, and had

The Nitehawks Dance Band in July 1954. They played at all the venues in Hatfield over the years. Dick Whittingham (far right), at the piano, still lives in Hatfield. (Ken Wright)

been in the Scouts over a year, we had a Scout troop of seventy-two. This was completely hopeless, because no way could you ever know the names or anything much about any of the boys, but we had seventy-two because of all the new families coming in.

Barrie Smith

The 20-35 Club

The 20-35 Club (a social club for people between those ages) moved their meeting place to The Breaks in 1951. We met two evenings a week for dances, discussions, lectures, indoor games, sports etc. and arranged outings. Jokers referred to it as the marriage bureau and at least thirty of us met our future spouses there, including me. The Hatfield Camera Club also met at the Breaks. Unfortunately for posterity we were a bit elitist and regarded the taking of local views as 'snapshotting'. In the Fifties and Sixties though, we did take all the current and past schools and churches in the area at the request of the local WEA. Membership started to fall when people had more money to spend on 'provided' leisure activities. We lost some of our more active members when the Hatfield Technical College started holding evening classes.

Reg Coleman

The Cycling Club

In the early Fifties the roads we know today did not exist, the New Towns were in the process of being built, new cars and finance were not too plentiful and petrol was still in short supply. This situation resulted in a fair number of people taking to the open road on bicycles. It was a somewhat familiar sight to see a well-organized club of up to twenty or more members cycling along the lanes and byways in our area. As part of the service to their members and cyclists in general, the CTC (Cyclists' Touring Club) appointed various catering establishments throughout the country to supply refreshments and lodging along the road. These would be mostly cafés and hotels on the main highways to private dwellings in towns and villages, offering facilities from cups of tea to bed and breakfast accommodation. These were listed in the club's handbook and were entered under the town and district. Thus for Hatfield in 1950 we have the following establishments: Merrythought Café, Great North Road (lunch, tea, supper and bath); alongside was the popular Marshmoor Café, which also was CTC appointed, and supplied teas and refreshments; North Mymms Old Maypole (lunch, tea, dinner and cups of tea); Brookmans Park Restaurant, 3 Great North Road (lunch, tea and supper).

Ron Kingdon

The cycle club used to come through Hatfield. They used to meet in the green hut in College Lane and Peter's Café that was the cycling centre.

The Swimming Pool

Apart from catering for the housing need, the Rural District Council tried to cater for recreation. The swimming pool was not very popular out in some of the villages, especially in Cuffley. 'Why should we pay for it? We

The town centre swimming pool under construction in 1965. (Sandy Ballard)

The 20-35 Club with their 'Roaring Twenties' tableau for the Hatfield Carnival in 1956. Reg Coleman is second from the left. (*Herts Advertiser*)

shall never get there to swim in it.' It was an innovative design, we actually got it remarkably cheaply, because it was anticipated that it would be successful, it would catch on and others like it would be built around the country. Unfortunately part of the way through the job the architect died, so that never happened. It was a very smart building in its day, it has one of those ingenious roofs that, despite all the curves, you can actually make the form-work for it out of straight boards. It provided an architectural stop at what was at that time one end of the town centre and gave us something that perhaps we are lacking in Hatfield. We don't have many buildings that you can say 'Well, that's a piece of architecture'.

Bill Storey

The Gosling Stadium

The Welwyn Hatfield District Council was responsible for providing the Gosling Stadium, which is just outside the Hatfield boundary by 200 yards. At that time, in 1959/60, we had a young lad living down Wellfield Road, Chris Church, who was a world-class cyclist. Chris and a young lad from Welwyn Garden City, Brendan McKeown, were two senior cyclists in this country. They appeared in a number of Olympics, and won some medals, but never a gold. Chris Church's name is the first one on the honours board at the Stadium.

Frank Clayton

The Marshmoor Café on Christmas Day, 1952. (Ken Wright)

The de Havilland Social Club

The de Havilland Social Club organized a wide range of activities for the employees. Every employee was required to contribute a small weekly subscription towards the cost of running the club. The main centre of the club's activities was the Club House which still stands today at the north end of the airfield site. This was built at the cost of the de Havilland Company. It included an assembly hall with a stage at one end. This was used as a dance hall and a theatre. There was also a snooker room with a number of tables. More than one bar was provided for the benefit of members. There were also a number of committee rooms for the meetings of the various societies. Changing rooms were also provided nearby for those indulging in athletic pursuits.

Regular visits were organized to London theatres. These included attendances at operas at Covent Garden or Sadlers Wells. A bus would leave the main gate at 5.30 p.m. as soon as the works closed, and would deliver the participants to the door of the theatre. It would be faithfully waiting for the return journey at the end of the performance. Each year the Social Club organized Christmas parties for the children of employees. Every child received a present at a splendid Christmas tea held in the works canteen. The climax of the social activities each year was Open Day which was held on the sports field near to Manor Road. There was always a fairground with the usual rides and stalls. The highlight of the day was the flying display, when as many de Havilland aircraft as possible would put on an impressive exhibition, including aerobatics which attracted crowds from miles around.

Departments were encouraged to organise displays illustrating the work in which they had been involved in the preceding year. Senior members of the staff would spend the day explaining to the many visitors the workings of their department. Everyone took great pride in their contribution to the company's success.

Frank Vann

Developing Interests

I think it was about 1960 when we decided to start a Gramophone Society. There were about forty members. We used to meet in Roe Hill House, where we placed the chairs in rows. I remember sometimes we had meetings at our house and we sat round the edge of the room. This was probably not a good idea, as some people chatted while the music was being played.

There were WEA lectures instigated by Dr and Mrs K Hutton. The ones that people remember best are the ones on the history of Hatfield, but I attended a series on music given by Eric Kohn in spring 1969. These were held in the Huttons' home at 2 Vigors Croft. There we sat in rows. Eric Kohn was an excellent speaker and the course was fascinating.

Janet Vann

Chess Club

One of the things that went on was the Chess Club, for a time one of the top four in the country, though I believe that it no longer exists. The first trophy was presented by Barbara Cartland and was the McCorquodale Trophy. It was played for on a knock-out basis. The trouble was that the same people tended to win it year after year, and with my well-known sense of fair play, I devised the idea of having a second trophy (which was actually a chess clock with a band around it for putting on the names of the winners). The idea was that you could only enter

A programme for the Finsbury Park Empire for May 1954. This venue was easily reached by train from Hatfield.

Donald Hodson, the Hilltop chemist, relaxes over a game of chess with the Hilltop Chess Club, April 1966. (Welwyn and Hatfield Times)

for the Hodson Trophy if you had not won either the McCorquodale or the Hodson already. So every year it was open to people who had not won anything. I thought that was a jolly good thing, because it opened it up to people who just knew they'd get slaughtered if they played some of the excellent players.

Donald Hodson

Mrs McCorquodale

Barbara Cartland (Mrs McCorquodale) got our Townswomen's Guild started. There was one in the Old Town but we didn't know about it at Roe Green, where we were all living. Then one of my friend's neighbours said that they were trying to start a second Townswomen's Guild. We were only in our twenties, and we thought, 'Townswomen's Guild?... They're old ladies'. This friend said, 'There's going to be a meeting which Mrs McCorquodale is going to take and it is to form a new Townswomen's Guild.' It was in Roe Hill House, and this friend said to me, 'Come on.' We went and Mrs McCorquodale was all dressed up in her party clothes, she said that she was going on to a party. We were quite thrilled, it was a sort of new world. Then she ended up saying that in two or three weeks' time she was going to give a cheese and wine party at the Cavendish Hall, and we were all invited. We went and she got some of her son's friends to do a revue; friends from Cambridge.

Janet Vann

A Good Sport

Mrs McCorquodale (Barbara Cartland) was a good sport, because I was involved in an amateur dramatics group in Welham Green. We wrote and asked if we could possibly have one of her old hats, and bless her cotton socks, she sent one. We were doing a play and we wanted someone in an elaborate hat. We said, 'Go on let's be devils'.

Maureen Cowie

The Women's Fellowship

We used to go to the Women's Fellowship with torches because there were no street lights. We used to meet in the little green hut in College Lane.

National Housewives' Register

The Hatfield branch was very active. It was a boon to mothers who wanted some intellectual stimulation as well as looking after babies. I particularly enjoyed the book review group and the play-reading sessions.

Shirley Knapp

Lots of Other Activities

There were lots of other activities going on, for example, I remember my wife being involved in Hatfield Drama and the local CND. There was a local consumer group, which I think existed almost before Which? magazine. The ladies used to tour the local shops and check the prices, carry

The Women's Institute stall in Hatfield Market. (Ron Kingdon)

out tests, and recommend pushchairs and things like this to one another. Hatfield Drama met in the original Oxlease Community Centre, if I remember correctly, and of course there's the Field View Club, that met in the Methodist Hall – that's still going as a rendezvous for the ladies. My wife and I ran a magazine circle, with Country Life, The Doctor, House and Garden, Illustrated London News and Autocar and circulated them. Members subscribed and we were responsible. You were allowed to keep the magazine for about a week or so, then pass it on, put on it a little list of initials, and pass it round. And if you had a particular interest in an article, and wanted to keep it later, you marked that and it went back to you.

Jim Parker

Other Dancing Venues

My favourite place for dancing was the Memorial Hall. I liked the Memorial Hall because I met all my friends there and we also belonged to a youth club and social club. Then when I went out with Tony we went to the Aircraft Factory. I met Tony at the Memorial Hall, although he was the boy next door. We used to meet on a Wednesday night and then it was Saturday night. Monday nights were at the social club. We had a friend of my brothers, who was in a band; he use to play at de Havilland's and we used to go. It was a lovely big band, all the brass in the front, and they used to stand up when they played. We went to the Technical College a

few times. We used to go there for New Year's Eve dances. They were great because you used to dress up! It was a real dressy do; dinner jackets for the men and long dresses for the ladies. We did have food there, but it wasn't a dinner dance where you sat down. It was a real night out!

Barbara Palmer

Scottish Dancing

About 1960 an evening class was started at Burleigh School to teach Scottish Country dancing. This was thoroughly enjoyable. The class was taken by Daisy Ord with her husband Ted helping. The Scottish music was supplied by a record player. It was mainly women who went, only a couple of men. Daisy and Ted encouraged us to go to Caledonian Society Balls at Harpenden and Welwyn Garden City. Unfortunately the class stopped after two years and we were all sad about it.

Janet Vann

Television and Radio

Before we had a TV of our own I remember being asked to watch the opera Eugene Onegin at a neighbour's house a bit further up Bishops Rise. Of course it was black and white in those days but it was so exciting to be able to watch an opera at home. When my children were growing up I wasn't much bothered about having a television.

I used to enjoy a lot of music and plays on the radio; listening to Women's Hour and the plays and serials. I remember hearing one particular series by David Kossoff when he was reading the Old Testament stories; it was wonderful.

Saturday Pocket Money

In the Fifties, when I was a child, I'd take my pocket money and walk along from my house to the nearest newsagents, which was called Drapers, in Birchwood, spend my money there and come back.

Pat Lewis

Saturday was Shopping

I suppose Saturday was shopping; it was a family activity and actually we used to come down to the public library after it was opened; it was quite a centre. We used to get a bus to the town centre. There was quite a good service from South Hatfield and sometimes we would walk to Hatfield Park after shopping.

Saturday was the day for shopping. The Green Line buses used to be full, taking people to London to the shops.

Michael Marlow and another

Up to London for the Day

Towards the 1960s our Saturdays never changed. Up at the crack of

Esther and Roderick Vann with the First World War tank in Hatfield Park during a Sunday afternoon walk in 1961. (Frank Vann)

dawn into the car and drive to Waterloo Bridge and park the car. We would wander around, look at museums and things, and then in the afternoon we would go to the ballet or to the theatre most Saturdays. It was so cheap you see. We only ever went in the gods or we had to stand. It was five shillings to stand at the back of the stalls at Covent Garden so we saw all the best ballets. It was wonderful. That was usually our Saturdays because I was working all the week. I was at de Havilland's from 1957 and I felt that Saturday was the children's day, so I took them out. If we didn't go to London we went somewhere else of interest but Sundays was housework from the crack of dawn until I fell into a bath at six o'clock in the evening.

Constance Schofield

We were Lucky we Had a Car

We were lucky we had a car. We took the children to London. We went to all the museums and sight-seeing an awful lot, because you could park easily in London in those days. I can remember up to the time we were married, we used to park in Pall Mall. That was easy on a Saturday but we used to park easily in a lot of places like Hyde Park, and then you were very near to the Albert Hall, the Science Museum, the Geological Museum and they were free.

Barbara Latham

The Treat of the Year

The treat of the year – we very rarely went out – was to go up to London on the one and threepence-halfpenny workman's train fare, and then we blew our money by having breakfast at the Marble Arch Corner House.

Walking at the Weekends

Saturday, in the summertime, we always went walking. Lots of families did and you met all sorts of people. The Oxlease estate was still being built and we were curious; we often used to go and walk in the new housing area and we walked along pipes and scaffolding to see what different houses were like.

June Smith

We used to walk at the weekend. We would go for a walk in Hatfield Park and the children used to play on the First World War tank that was there. There would be children climbing all over it. We also took our children to a park by Hollier's Dairies (the Recreation Ground) and went to walk over to Colney Heath from Hazel Grove across the old A1. We used to go a lot into what's now the University grounds. There was far more open space there then and we were able to go in and gather mushrooms; there were all sorts there.

Anne Dunkley

Saturday Evenings

Saturdays in the evenings was always the radio. It could be a play or it could be a variety show. We were all very keen on drama and we always listened to plays.

Constance Schofield

Cinema in Hatfield

The new building changed hands many times, becoming the Odeon on 7 October 1946, the Classic on 17 December 1967, the Curzon on 16 February 1969 and the Chequers on 16 April 1969. The last owners ran films on certain days and Bingo on others, until the final curtain came down on Saturday 2 June 1973 with the last major film, The Godfather.

Ron Kingdon

Back Row of the Cinema

In the Sixties, in the evening it was my courting days so it would be in the back row of the old Odeon cinema, night after night.

Pat Lewis

We Formed a Cinema Club

In the early days people like Harold Duckworth, myself and others, formed a cinema club and hired films. I think Harold owned a projector and a screen, and we used to hire the big

room at Hilltop, and show sort of art films like The Seven Samurai. They were all very worthy films that didn't often come up at the commercial cinema; it was quite successful.

Donald Hodson

CHAPTER 8

Schooldays and Moving On

The start of the summer holidays for Gascoyne Cecil School, July 1960. (*Welwyn and Hatfield Times*)

Junior School Looked so Big

The junior school (Broad Oaks) always looked so big when we were infants. I remember doing writing and maths and reading the 'Janet and John' books. We had PE in the hall with skipping ropes, in our vest and pants and barefoot. In the playground we played skipping games, marbles, played on the 'white bar' and did handstands against the wall.

Janet Howard

Howe Dell

We went on lots of nature walks to Stream Woods. The art room was over the cloakrooms, which used to be stables. We did lots of clay and painting, and also cookery – all in the same room. We also did lots of sewing: I remember sitting on the iron steps of the fire escape outside the sewing room, and talking as well as sewing. There were big stone flags in the hall, and a huge fireplace, a big, high-ceilinged brewery, a library, a music room, and little attic rooms used for storage. Outside was a huge cedar tree with crocuses round it, and a pond where someone's dad put a boat and we learned to row. When I was in the fourth year juniors, we put on a play of Tom Sawyer out on the green by the mulberry tree and I was the cross aunt. There was a huge tree as you came in the gate too where an owl nested and we found pellets underneath it containing the bones of what it had eaten.

Jacky Glanville

A Camel of Snow

Miss Matthews was our head teacher, she was quite strict and I think she was a perfectionist. She was very proud of her school, and liked to show off all the good things we could do. We did lots of concerts outside on a bank that was like a stage. I think history was her favourite subject; I remember doing lots of things about the Elizabethans. She got very excited the day the decorators found an old painting on the wall in the library, I think it was of an old country fair with a dancing bear. I went on many school trips to museums and other places. We used to do PE in our pants and vest. I don't think we had any big equipment, just beanbags, balls, and ropes. We also did a lot of country dancing, and I used to hate getting a partner with sweaty hands. We also had a big climbing frame in the enclosed playground that we used for PE. We had to go down a hill for that. Each class took turns to play on it at playtime. I don't ever remember tennis nets being up in the playground but there were the holes for the posts that we used for playing marbles. I remember playing conkers and cat's cradle, and a lot of chasing games and skipping. In the winter we made some really good slides on the ice, especially on the sloping piece of ground just in front of the school. One very cold winter, our class made a camel out of snow, on the playing field, that was big enough for two or three children to sit on. It lasted for ages after the snow had melted.

Teresa Brummel (née Smith)

Frequent French Lessons

One thing I remember very clearly from junior school (Gascoyne Cecil) is that we had frequent French lessons, for at least the last two years. We would listen to a tape-recording and then the whole class would repeat it. Towards the end of the lesson we would draw a picture in our books with a French sentence underneath. When the book was completed it told a story in French. Great emphasis was put on French lessons at this school. In our last year (1969) the school was chosen to make a film about teaching French to be shown to teachers. The whole class rehearsed for the film many times and the head of French Education in Hertfordshire visited several times, including the day the filming took place in our class. Filming went very well except for one thing. I was the only person in the whole class to make a mistake. But the head of French Education said this was good because I had corrected the mistake myself and she also complimented me on my accent!

Sally

Never Mind the Spelling

My children went to Green Lanes School and one of the teachers, or maybe it was school policy, did not teach times tables. My husband had arguments because he was emphatic that they should be taught their tables. The policy then was, that they were taught them by using them and that the children would gradually learn them

like that. I don't think that was the right way and when it came to English composition, spelling didn't matter and I think that was wrong. It was getting the quantity down as much as you could on the paper, never mind the spelling.

Barbara Latham

You Must Never Correct

I had great problems because I went to teacher training college in 1965 and I was horrified. I did it, I got my teaching certificate, but I didn't believe what I was doing, because you must never tell a child something was wrong, you must never correct anything. This was in the junior school. No, I didn't last.

Maureen Cowie

The Idea was the Thing

You were told that the 'idea' was the thing rather than the presentation, and of course we had been brought up on stating the case as it were and expounding your reply. You were told that punctuation and grammar didn't matter one jot, as long as the idea was got across. To some extent I felt that wasn't too bad because it meant that ideas weren't held back by expression, but I think that maybe the education system went a little too far then. The idea was good, but the application wasn't so good and really didn't apply to all pupils either.

Watching the First Moon Landing

At Millwards School in July 1969, just before the end of the summer term, we were all ushered into the darkened hall, the doors of the large TV screen were opened, and we saw what must have been a recording of the first moon landing, on the previous day. First a blurred image of a lunar module leg and some moon dust, then after what seemed a very long wait, Neil Armstrong emerged and carefully descended the ladder to utter that mistakenly worded phrase, 'That's one small step for man, one giant leap for mankind'. I did a project on space, and wrote to NASA. They sent me an impressive, glossy brochure. Another day we were told we would be going outside to see the eclipse – partial – of the sun. I vividly remember our teachers providing smoked glass, exposed photographic film, and pinhole camera devices for us to safely observe the event. I'm not sure everyone grasped the concept of bodies in motion, but it was a memorable day.

David Parker

Staniforth School of Dancing

In the Fifties and Sixties the Staniforth School of Dancing used the first floor rooms above the Co-op food store (near the old bus garage, on the corner of St Albans Road and Beaconsfield Road). There were ballet classes on Mondays

The old police station in St Albans Road East, September 1969. The man on the bicycle is Tom Padget, the headmaster of Countess Anne School. (English Partnerships/Ken Wright)

Summer Fête at Dellfield School, June 1962. (*Welwyn and Hatfield Times*/Denis J. Williams)

and tap and American rhythm on Wednesday. You entered by a dark staircase at the side of the building, and at the top on the right there were dressing rooms and waiting rooms. On the left was the dance studio with wall bars and a piano, played always, it seemed, by Mrs Hill.

My sister and I walked to our classes from the 'shops' end of Crawford Road, taking various routes to Ground Lane, avoiding fierce dogs at the top of the road, and after buying a supply of sweets (2oz of pineapple chunks) from Drapers, the post office on Birchwood Avenue. Mrs Staniforth, the Principal, was a lightly built, energetic, enthusiastic teacher who demanded very high standards, could be fearsome at times and, in the ten years I attended, never seemed to change or grow any older.

We were entered for ballet and tap examinations to gain certificates and medals, and these took place in the studio with an external examiner from the Royal Academy of Dancing. Here I have memories of nervous anticipation, of fear that hair or dress were not correct, of a seemingly endless wait for the results and of disappointment at only achieving passes, never merits or distinctions.

More enjoyable were the many concerts for charity. The first ones I remember were to celebrate war victories and took place in the Public Hall near the station. Other venues included Wellfield Home, the Memorial Halls (old and new), church halls and various schools, including the newly built Gascoyne Cecil School. One of the highlights was the performance in the Old Palace Gardens in front of the Queen Mother to celebrate the Festival of Britain.

Pat Lewis

Talking about Hatfield School

My first day there, I was scared and very nervous. Although only two miles away, Welham Green seemed a different world from Hatfield. I was coming from a village school where everyone knew everyone, to a school where I knew almost no-one. There were four classes for first year, and we were divided up alphabetically. I was in 1F, the forms were named after scientists, reflecting the science basis of the school; D for Darwin, F for Faraday, N for Newton, and R for Rutherford. I must have been a little late, because I remember there being only one empty desk, next to a girl. Her name was Sharon and we became best friends all through school. There were only seven girls in the class; the boys outnumbered us two to one.

Alison Cowie

THE ROYAL ACADEMY OF DANCING INCORPORATED BY ROYAL CHARTER
154 Holland Park Avenue, London, W.11 PATRON : HER MAJESTY THE QUEEN

CANDIDATE'S NAME   Patricia Burns

PLEASE ATTEND AT   Co-Operative Hall St.Albans Road
                              Hatfield.

ON Thursday, 10th December 1953

Bring   AT   5.45 p.m
this card
with you as you cannot be examined without it

Important :
For rules concerning examination attendance, P.T.O.

GENERAL REMARKS :

make the *fondu* softer in *plies fondu*
Keep the Shoulders down when arms are raised in *2es: ex:*
Patricia must work for more co-ordination of arms & feet.
Character steps were poor.

EXAMINER   *Ethel. M. Moore.*

BALLET IN EDUCATION

CHILDREN'S EXAMINATIONS IN DANCING

Grade Five

Technique and Theory throughout	30	18
Sense of Movement, Music and Rhythm	30	19
Deportment, Expression and Presentation throughout	20	14
Dances H 20, N 7, 7	20	14
Total	100	65

TOTAL IN WORDS   Sixty Five

RESULT —
HONOURS   85
COMMENDED   75
PASSED   65

NO CORRESPONDENCE CAN BE ENTERED INTO REGARDING THE RESULT OF THIS EXAMINATION

Left: Pat Lewis (*née* Burns) and Carole Payne (*née* Burns) in the gardens of the Old Palace at Hatfield House, June 1951. (Pat Lewis)
Right: Pat Lewis' dance examination certificate, December 1953. (Pat Lewis)

Everyone Learnt an Instrument

One of the many great things about Hatfield School was that Dr Hutton made every first-year pupil learn a musical instrument and also learn to swim. My son went on from there to the Royal Academy of Music. When I hear my grandson of eleven years playing Dr Hutton's instrument, the bassoon, (and also the flute, piccolo, guitar and piano), I thank God for the influence of Hatfield School. One of the teachers in my son's time, Dorothy Harrison, used to bring the school bass to our house until we bought him his own instrument, so that he could practice in the holidays.

Pat Glanville

A Very Experimental Institution

I came as a teacher to Hatfield School. Hatfield School was then taking in its second tranche of teachers, it had just got a sixth form for the first time. It was a school called a 'technical high school', which meant that it wasn't a grammar school, and it wasn't a secondary modern school, and nobody quite knew what a technical high school was. So it was a very experimental institution and it was very good fun to work in. We were all about thirty years of age, all the teachers and it was a very thrilling thing to do. It was, also strangely enough, quite a rarity in those days for men to teach girls. Co-education was still a comparatively new idea; in fact the very term co-educational is dead as a

Pupils leaving Hatfield Technical High School in the grounds of the Hatfield Technical College (now the University of Hertfordshire), June 1965. The name changed later to Hatfield School and it eventually moved to new premises in South Hatfield. (English Partnerships/Ken Wright)

doornail, because nowadays you always expect schools to be 'mixed sex' which I suppose is how we describe them now. But then it was a comparatively new idea in England so that the whole thing, the school, newly built, and the youth of the staff, and this whole new town, was like going on to another planet.

David Cregan

I studied all the normal subjects in the first two years, including German. In the first year the girls spent a term doing woodwork and metalwork, whilst the boys did cookery. I made a tea towel holder with a marble in it, a fruit bowl in woodwork and enamelled brooches and pendants in metalwork. By the third year we had chosen our subjects for O levels. I did English Language, Literature, Maths, Geography, History, Physics, Art, Domestic Science, Needlework, German and French. In the sixth form I did Economics O level, and A levels in Maths, English, and Economics.

Teresa Brummel (née Smith)

Parent-teacher Meetings

We have always had a good spirit in Hatfield regarding education, we've been very fortunate in what's been provided for us. I think the attendance at parent-teacher meetings and the like has shown that – at Hatfield School they just went on all night.

Jim Parker

The Girls' Grammar School

The school was good for science, I think because the headmistress, Miss Ashworth, was a chemist. When we had to choose our GCE options at the end of the third year; we had to do at least one science, which I didn't like (though in fact I liked the Chemistry with Mrs Pryce), but which was quite enlightened for girls at that time. School assembly took place every day, a reading probably from the Bible, (sometimes I read, but it was nerve racking), a hymn, ('Morning has broken', 'I vow to thee my country', etc.), a prayer (the Ignatius Loyola one) and notices. But on Fridays, each form took a turn at presenting something, and I remember one where we listened to the pop record 'With God on Our Side'. Girls at a grammar school either went to university, to teacher training college, or (because Miss Ashworth was a scientist) were allowed to work in a hospital as a radiographer or whatever. When I said I wanted to work in the theatre, they said 'Yes, yes, now what do you really want to do?' It was suggested I needed another string to my bow, and they persuaded me to train to teach drama. Later, I may have been in the sixth form, I produced a one-act play by N.F. Simpson, and the whole school was made to watch!

Jackie Glanville

Attracted by the Pleated Skirt

My son went to Hatfield School and my daughter to the Girls' Grammar School. I was not keen on

4 THE PARADE, ST. ALBANS ROAD   20 GT. NORTH ROAD
HATFIELD, Herts.
Tel.: Hatfield 3165

RICHARDSON'S
(Mrs. P. WHITE)
Children's Outfitter
Ladies' Wear   Knitting Wool
We close at 1 o'clock on Thursdays

M............................ August 20th 1962

Item	£	s	d
Skirt		3	1	6
2 Blouses @ 21/6		2	3	0
Tie			9	6
Belt			5	6
Knickers 2 @ 6/11			13	10
Beret			13	11
Sports Blouse			15	6
2 pr Socks 3/4			7	10
Raincoat		6	13	6
			17	9
		16	1	10
			15	9
5521		16	17	7

RECEIVED WITH THANKS

A receipt for school uniform for Janet Vann's daughter, who was attending Hatfield Girls' Grammar School (now Bishop's Hatfield Girls' School). (Janet Vann)

single-sex schools, but my daughter was attracted by the pleated skirt which was part of the uniform, and my husband thought that they would turn out 'little ladies'. Well, we all make mistakes, don't we?

Pat Glanville

German Exchange

In 1953 when I was a schoolboy I went on one of these exchange visits to Germany and stayed with a family there. This family was obviously well-heeled and on a Sunday evening the whole family went out to a restaurant, probably the first time I ever went out to a restaurant. When we sat down at the table there was a big pat of butter on the table, probably about half a pound of butter, and my eyes must have popped out of my head. The lady whom I was staying with said to me, 'What's the matter? It's only butter', and I replied, 'Well it's probably as much as I see in a month,' and there it was on the table of the restaurant in Germany. Her reply was, 'But we lost the war'.

Brian Lawrence

You Walked to School

I walked to school and we had great fun with Mrs Pike the lollipop lady. We used to march up to her and salute, and when she retired we were asked to give a present to her.

You walked. You walked doing the shopping, you walked to town, the children walked to and from school.

I used to walk my daughter to school, but when I had my sons I used to have a little seat on the bicycle, because it used to save time ... In those days you could let the children walk to school unaccompanied whereas you can't nowadays.

In fact if you saw a car pull up outside a school in those days you'd think something serious had happened.

Teresa Brummel, Anne Dunkley and others

Building Schools

When the schools were originally built on Woods Avenue and Travellers Lane, it was a dead end. In the late Sixties it was still a muddy track and we felt secure in that our children were going to school on that road. Subsequently that end was opened up to the Southern Link road

The Inter-Schools Football Cup Final in March 1964, between North Mymms Junior School and Gascoyne Cecil School. Terry Medwin of Tottenham Hotspur FC presents the cup to the captain of Gascoyne Cecil, who won 1-0. The match was played at Newtown School, Hatfield. (Ron Kingdon)

and it's now become a through route for quite heavy traffic. I really thought that was a sensible concept, to put schools to which children would walk along a dead end road. Suddenly it's all open. Of course we had the Woods Avenue/Travellers Lane Protest Group and as a result we got at least one or two subways. These are rarely used now of course, because people are worried about the subways and what goes on in them.

Jim Parker

Career Guidance

My daughter was interested in science and biology and she got virtually no career advice. They hadn't a clue where to look for something for a girl to do in realms of science.

As it turned out, I did not go to university, but found myself a job as a laboratory technician at the Imperial Cancer Research Fund in London.

Maureen and Alison Cowie

Work Experience

It was Easter 1950 and my sister Pamela stayed on a term to get her City and Guilds exam and she did a week's work experience over at the Propeller Company. She did not get paid for it. At about the same time Sir Geoffrey de Havilland and the chairman, Mr Butler, regularly took children who were about to leave school for a tour of the factory. The important thing was that the kids saw the factory in working conditions, in its natural mucky state, not like most people in Hatfield who only saw it on Open Days when it had been done up as if for a royal visit. They used to start cleaning up on Monday and they were still chasing like hell to get it cleaned up by four o'clock on Friday afternoon.

David Willson

I think there must have been different banks, factories or other firms who agreed to come into the scheme. I remember my daughter went to Barclays one day and was there at nine o'clock, was taken in and shown around and what went on. Obviously they couldn't handle money, or work at the counter, but it gave them an insight into what the work was like.

Barbara Latham

Evening and Day Release

I used to go up one evening a week, from here to London to Regent Street Polytechnic. I used to do that every Monday night after I'd left work. I was an apprentice to a local hairdresser in Hatfield. I used to get back here about eleven at night and I was allowed an hour off to go at five o'clock. I paid my own fare, but she paid my fees for me.

Joyce Chapman

When my husband came to Hatfield Tech, he had done his

degree during the war but he'd only made it through a Pass degree, so he decided he'd like to do an Honours degree, so he did that, I think at Regent Street Poly. Hatfield Technical College were not prepared to give him any time off at all, and he needed a day. He was already working one evening a week so he had to do extra evenings to make up for that day. He then did an MSc after that and again got no time. Now you get a year off to do things like that. He did it all in his own time with a young family.

Engineering Apprentices

You did 'day release' and if you had been upgraded to 'Engineering Apprentice' and declared an interest in a specialization, they took steps to enable that to happen. Your moves around the works would follow a particular pattern and you would end your 'time' in the department of your choice. You had the same rights, in fact, as a student but because a de Havilland student paid money, he could choose, to some extent, what he did. Most of them liked to work on the aeroplanes, rather than the bits and pieces.

Jim Parker

No Holiday without Night School

I worked for Nortmet Engineering, pre-war and post-war. Pre-war I was just an assistant and they didn't pay

Frank Clayton in 1962. He was a councillor for Hatfield Rural District Council and a school governor. (Welwyn and Hatfield Times)

you for your holidays unless you went to night school. You had to get 80 per cent and you had to get your certificate signed by the teacher and hand it in to your boss to get your pay for your holidays.

Ron Kingdon

CHAPTER 9

Getting There

The junction of Mill Green Lane with the Hertford Road at Mill Green before the A1000 road linking Welwyn Garden City and Hatfield was constructed, October 1963. (English Partnerships/Ken Wright)

Ron Kingdon in 1965. (Ron Kingdon)

End of an Era

With the coming to an end of the steam era the Hatfield shed closed on 2 January 1961; the Hertford branch was closed in May 1967. Apart from the general traffic they had brought to the main line – orchids, bananas and coal on the St Albans feeder, straw hats and associated goods from Luton and malt and barley to and from Hertford – each of the lines had its own little niche in local history. The Salvation Army's press in Camp Road, St Albans, was responsible for the printing of their paper The War Cry which was distributed through the world. The many thousands of bundles of this production started the first leg of their journey in closed goods wagons on the St Albans branch to Hatfield.

Ron Kingdon

It Seemed a Very Long Journey

We had to travel by train to visit relatives who lived in Wood Green and Finsbury Park and also to go on holiday, before we had the car. Our first holiday in 1954 was to Winchelsea Beach in Sussex. We walked to Hatfield station, carrying cases, and caught a train to London. We then had to cross London by Tube to get to the terminal for Winchelsea, which was probably Victoria or Waterloo – I can't remember. It seemed a very long journey and we were very tired when we got there. It rained for most of the fortnight.

Watching the Flying Scotsman

By the late Sixties steam trains had gone out of regular use on the main London-Edinburgh line, which passed

The *Flying Scotsman* on a ceremonial run, passing through Welwyn Garden City and shortly to pass through Hatfield, May 1968. (Ken Wright)

the bottom of our school field. One day at about 11 o'clock we were all taken outside to see the Flying Scotsman steam engine come through. What a splendid sight, sound and smell, with its shiny green paint and brass, as it sped past with whistle shrieking – a 'living, breathing beast', not the dull machine like the Deltic diesels we saw every day.

David Parker

A Proper Station

Hatfield used to have a proper station. I was interested in all the signals, good old mechanical ones known as Semaphores which flopped up and down. Nowadays they have electric signals that don't work.

The Bus Drivers Rushed Off

I used to go down to the railway station with the children to pick up my husband. There was a waiting room, a little café place in those days, which the bus drivers used to sit in and drink cups of tea. We used to laugh, because just before the trains were due all the bus drivers rushed off and got in their buses before the people got off the train.

Anne Dunkley

Parcels Delivered to the Station

In the Sixties one still got parcels delivered to the railway station and you were informed that there was a parcel awaiting collection. You went down to the parcel office to collect. The porter was a very pleasant man, you could also send items from there.

Ron Kingdon

The Driver Waited for Regulars

There was a railway line from St Albans to Hatfield. A passenger train ran twice a day. The driver would wait a minute or two to pick up regulars. There was also the daily 'banana train' at 5.40 a.m.

The Fire in the Waiting Room

I remember when the station waiting rooms had log fires and sitting in the waiting room at Hatfield with a lovely fire.

'Hang On'

In October 1967 whilst making a record on film of the Hatfield to Smallford section of the St Albans to Hatfield branch line, I arrived at the East Hyde level crossing to picture the one freight train a day around 8.30 a.m. The train arrived from Hatfield which would become the 'Banana Special' on its return journey from Smallford. The gates were opened and the diesel loco and vans crossed Ellenbrook Lane. Due to the fact this was the only train, I was hoping to record the event on back and white and colour slide stock, as well as to achieve some of the movement on cine film. For one person to do this alone was virtually impossible. When the train had passed over, one of the crew asked if I had managed to get my pictures. I replied that I had, but wished to record the scene using the cine camera. 'Hang on' he said 'and I will reverse the train back over the crossing for the retake of your film'. This was duly done, the level crossing gates closed behind the re-run train, and thanks to the helpfulness of British Rail personnel the event was recorded for

The 'Banana Special' at Nast Hyde Halt, October 1967. (Ron Kingdon)

The Wrestlers' Bridge collapse over the main-line railway, 20 February 1966. (Ron Kingdon)

posterity. No doubt waiting motorists must have been wondering what was going on!

Ron Kingdon

Serious Matters

On such a well used railway as the GNR's route to the north, mishaps are bound to happen at some stage. Hatfield was fortunately spared from major disasters, but one incident comes to mind. On the morning of 20 February 1966 the old Wrestlers Bridge, built in 1850, collapsed on to the track of the 'up' line. With two trains having previously passed through only quick action by workers on the line prevented further trains running. Luckily too, no vehicles were on the road overhead and no lives were lost.

On 11 February 1952 the funeral train of the late George VI left Kings Lynn in Norfolk for its journey to Kings Cross, hauled by a specially chosen Pacific Britannia British Railways standard class 7 locomotive, N.70000. The train was made up of ex-LNER teak coaches with a first class saloon No. 46, painted black for the occasion and carrying the coffin. The train would have passed through Hatfield station around 2 p.m., with many residents watching from the platform and along the route.

Ron Kingdon

Cycling

The first Principal of the College, Dr Chapman, used a bicycle for transport, later upgrading to an auto-cycle (a forerunner of the motor scooter). A party from the 20-35 Club had arranged to be shown over the Technical School before it opened. We were waiting outside for someone to meet us and we saw this figure cycling across the car park towards us. We thought, 'Here comes the caretaker to open up,' but it was Dr Chapman come to show us around!

Reg Colman

Bill Salmon

Bill Salmon (the Youth and Community worker) for years resisted buying a car. He said that travelling around the town on a bike he met more people, including parents, to stop and talk to.

Reg Coleman

My Dad Used to Cycle

My dad used to cycle in the evening when it was dark to meet me, because I was at the Hatfield Technical College and it was a little country lane

Cycling proficiency tests at Dellfield School, August 1962. PC Lester is checking a bicycle. (*Welwyn and Hatfield Times*/Denis J. Williams)

up to there and there were no lamp posts.

Shirley Knapp

The Bus to Southend

A bus came down Hazel Grove to a lay-by between our road and Willow Way, with Southend on its indicator window. As the weather was nice, I packed Christine's bucket and spade and a picnic, and we boarded this bus. When I asked for a return to Southend, the conductor said 'You are here'. I felt a real fool, but we went along Bishops Rise, up a path by the Water Board, which was only a hut then, to a lovely open space with a sandpit.

Jessie Axford

There was the 340 going up to South Hatfield, but they called it South End

and it caused a lot of concern to the people who'd moved up from London who truly got on it thinking they were going to Southend. The name was later changed to 'South Hatfield'.

June Smith

The Buses were on Time

Buses used to be on time. The Green Line used to arrive and you argued with the driver if it was half a minute early or half a minute late. Its regularity was quite incredible.

The buses were on time. I used to get the 9.20 at the Stonehouse and that was twenty minutes past nine unless there had been a tragedy en route. If we had thick fog, they used to give up sometimes. They used to get to Barnet and the drivers would give up there because they were exhausted after miles of creeping along unlit roads.

A No. 303 bus waiting outside the old bus garage in St Albans Road East. (Michael Rooum)

Waters Garage on Brewery Hill, Old Hatfield, where Brian Lawrence bought his scooter, March 1967. (English Partnerships/Ken Wright)

Come on, It's your Stop!

We used to fall asleep and they would wake us up. On the journey home going back to London, after working nights here, you'd just fall asleep and you'd get shaken up at Golders Green: 'Come on, it's your stop!'

Jim Parker

The Conductor who Knitted

There was a conductor who used to do knitting on the 303. He used to sit on the bench seat and do the most elaborate knitting.

The Bridge Took off the Top

I knew many of the drivers of the double-decker buses. I remember one of them who wanted to go home before he went back to Hatfield Garage. To go home he went underneath the bridge in Wellfield Road and the bridge took off the top of the double-decker bus. Nobody was injured, fortunately, but the driver got his knuckles rapped!

Frank Clayton

Hatfield was of Some Importance

Hatfield was obviously considered of some importance, as for example in the 1960s the de Havilland (British Aerospace) factory and site were served by four bus routes (303, 330, 340, 341). Likewise Hatfield Technical College, as it was known then, was privileged with no less than six bus routes (303, 315A, 330, 340B, 340C, 341) while Green Lanes School had the 330 service. A number of these journeys were not listed in the normal timetables.

Ron Kingdon

The Posh Way Round

From Birchwood Avenue towards Welwyn Garden City, the 303 used to go round the back, round the poor way and the fare was threepence. If you went the posh way round Valley Road, it was fourpence.

Frank Clayton

Got the Sunday Buses Going

Our parish priest at St Peter's was Father Milne. He was the one who got Sunday buses going, because there were no buses on a Sunday until the afternoon.

Anne Dunkley

Honeymoon in an Austin A 30

A few days before we were going to get married, we had a Morris Series E and something major happened to it, so we couldn't use it to go down to Torquay for our honeymoon. We were going to borrow my mother's little Austin A 30, but there was a problem with the petrol tank. During the ceremony and during the reception, the petrol tank was being worked on, but that the first night of my honeymoon was spent in an Austin A 30.

Pat Lewis

No MOTs in Those Days

All cars were going for export well into the '50s; there was even a restriction on the number of new cars. There were priority categories – I think only doctors. It was a bit like houses, you had to have so many points to purchase a new car. There were an awful lot of old cars on the road. I had one myself, a van with windows cut in it to save on tax. I remember coming up to the building site and the door came off. There were no MOTs in those days!

We Had a Morris Minor

We had a Morris Minor in the 1960s. Norman sold it many years ago, but it still comes back to Hatfield and quite often Norman comes dashing in 'I've seen our Morris Minor!' He chats to the owner who belongs to the Morris Minor club.

Shirley Knapp

My Volkswagen Beetle

The first car I had was in '64; it was a Volkswagen Beetle. It was old, second-hand and a had a very small rear window, and the only instrument it had on its dashboard was a speedometer, nothing else, no petrol gauge, nothing.

Hillman winners

THE NEW HILLMAN MINX DE LUXE SALOON

The car with the look-ahead look. Contemporary yet distinguished lines outside, improved seating inside. The powerful 1600 c.c. engine for brisk economical motoring The added plus of FRONT DISC BRAKES and NO GREASING POINTS! Servicing is only required every 3000 miles. Think how maintenance costs are cut. Borg-Warner automatic transmission available as an optional extra. Price £634. 18. 9 (incl. P.T.)

HILLMAN IMP

An inspiration in light car design. 875 c.c. overhead-camshaft engine gives a comfortable 75 m.p.h., a touring fuel consumption of 40–45 m.p.g. Standard model £508. 1. 3. (incl. P.T.) De luxe model £532. 4. 7. (incl. P.T.)

HILLMAN HUSKY – ANOTHER HILLMAN WINNER

Tough – vigorous – versatile. Dual-purpose family saloon or rugged load carrier. Price: £586. 12. 1. (incl. P.T.)

HILLMAN SUPER MINX

Greater economy, smoother running, improved carburation, and higher rear axle ratio. Borg-Warner automatic transmission available as an optional extra.
Prices: Saloon £743. 13. 9. (incl. P.T.) Convertible £849. 19. 6. (incl. P.T.) Estate £798. 1. 3. (incl. P.T.)

H.P. TERMS

Lowest possible deposit. Balance over three years.

PART EXCHANGE

terms all part of the Waters service.

WATERS

Known for good service since 1896

BY-PASS, HATFIELD. Tel: 4521 Branches at: 3–9 North Road, Hertford. Tel. 3044. 30 Stonehills, Welwyn Garden City. Tel. 25033

ROOTES DISTRIBUTORS IN HERTFORDSHIRE

An advertisement for Waters Garage from 1963. They still have a dealership in the same location, although the road is now named Comet Way.

You had to double de-clutch to get through the gears as well – that was great fun. You did have a lever under the dashboard somewhere, and if you ran out of petrol you pulled that and you had one gallon in a reserve tank. Never enjoyed motoring so much since.

At Every Road Junction I Stalled

I bought my first vehicle in 1957 when I was doing my National Service. It was a Lambretta scooter which I bought at Waters down in the Old Town at Hatfield. I lived on the Great North Road just north of The Wrestlers. At the garage they said, 'You do this, you do this, you do this,' and I didn't understand a thing about it. I didn't have the nerve to turn right, drive up the Great North Road past the station, over the railway bridge and down to where I lived. I turned left and left again into Park Street, along Park Street out onto the Old Hertford Road, round Mount Pleasant, out at Jack Olding's and came down the Great North Road to get home. And at every road junction I stalled it, no one had told me you had to de-clutch at a road junction and that was my first experience of taking charge of a vehicle on the road. I had it for about eighteen months and fell off it several times on icy mornings. I then decided to buy my first car which was an old Ford Popular, a secondhand 'sit up and beg', with three forward gears and one reverse. I felt much safer with four wheels. I think the Lambretta only took half a gallon and I used to fill up at Grays Garage with this two stroke mixture and a shot of Red X or something, for half a crown. The Lambretta cost me I think £150, which I bought on hire purchase and the car cost me £290. My dad gave me £200 towards it.

Brian Lawrence

Road Changes

The collapse of the bridge carrying the Great North Road over the railway isolated The Wrestlers from much of the town and stimulated the road changes which led to Salisbury Square.

I get very muddled if anybody asks me where such and such a road is now.

Ellenbrook Lane was accessible then to the A1. The A405 to Hatfield and Watford was rarely used. People practised driving along it. The Poly – now University – was open ground. I can't remember how many times the way round the Comet Hotel has changed. I can remember in the summer of 1952 sitting on a seat facing the Comet with my daughter in her pram while I was reading an enthralling book. There wasn't the traffic then.

Peggy Jones and another

First Trip by Air

Our first trip in an aeroplane was around 1969 or 1970 and we went to Ibiza from Luton. We took off in late evening and arrived at our hotel around 2 a.m. I remember quite enjoying the plane trip – it was a new experience for me and I was impressed with the meal we were served during the flight.

My first flight must have been the end of the '50s, I think, with two former college friends and we were going to do a tour of North France and one of us had just acquired a car so she was taking it on the aeroplane car ferry. We went from Lydd to Le Touquet and there were about six or eight passengers. We went about the speed of a bicycle so you saw the ships in the Channel underneath you.

Going to Jersey in an Old Dakota

I went to Jersey in '57 in an old Dakota. I got myself so worked up, so excited I was physically sick the day before – it was incredible. And coming back we had to

The 1st Hatfield Scouts with leader Mr Chubb Coleman about to depart for Jersey, August 1960. (*Welwyn and Hatfield Times*)

change from the aircraft to another one because they thought there was a Colorado beetle on it and you see that was deadly to vegetation.

Barbara Latham

Somebody's Left a Window Open!

We were flying across the Med and my wife's one of those women who always feels a draught. She'll find and feel a draught anywhere at all, no matter how. The draught will always find her and she was shivering on this plane, 'Go up the front,' she said, 'I think somebody's left a window open.'

Frank Clayton

Going on Holiday

We used to tow a caravan down to Devon and we always stopped at Rodborough Fort which is just above Stroud. It's very high up. I don't know how many counties you can see but quite a few and the children used to slide on cardboard boxes down the banks. We always stopped there on the way down and again on the way back and we spent two weeks down in Devon. We used to get the children up about five o'clock in the morning and they'd be fast asleep. We put them in the back of the car because those days you could take quite a few people in the car without seat belts. We used to stop somewhere and have breakfast and then

Cavendish Way Bridge in October 1958. It was later demolished to make way for the A1(M) tunnel development. (English Partnerships/Ken Wright)

they'd get dressed and we'd go on from there.

The Car had Four Bald Tyres

I can remember going down to Fowey in Cornwall with a friend of mine with our two wives and two kids and we were working at Mulhead's together then. We hired a car, it was something you did in those days – there weren't all the hire firms that there are now. We were about to hire it but the night before we were about to pick it up, it was no longer available for reasons I can't remember. But somebody knew somebody who knew somebody who could go and get a car the following morning. When we picked it up, I did not drive then, Geoff was the driver, he looked at the car and he nearly wept at the condition of it. The fact that it had four bald tyres didn't make us very happy at all. Anyway, after a long string of problems, we got down to Fowey just in

time to put it in the garage and pick it up a week later to come home again. In those days everyone went on holiday on a Saturday and came home on Saturday. As we were coming up a steep hill there was traffic for miles and miles, somebody kept flashing. We couldn't understand why because we were creeping along so slowly. Geoff hadn't noticed we'd got a flat tyre. But way up this hill we eventually got the message and got out and had a look and nearly died. Then, from nowhere at all, two policemen just dropped out of the sky like that! Geoff, my pal, nearly fainted in case they saw the bald tyres. They said, 'Can't give a bugger about that as long as we get you over that hill.' And I have got a photograph of those two policemen changing the tyre!

Frank Clayton

CHAPTER 10

Christmas

Mrs Hugh McCorquodale (Dame Barbara Cartland) helps Mrs Annie Clibbon, aged ninety-seven, to cut the Christmas cake at Wellfield Hospital, December 1962. (*Welwyn and Hatfield Times*/Denis J. Williams)

Christmas in our Own Home

Before the children were born, we always decided we'd have Christmas in our own home and we had the tradition of going off to the midnight mass, coming back and opening our presents then. But then, after the children were born, that wasn't practical anymore, so we had a tradition of opening our presents after we'd been to church and before we had Christmas dinner. I found this awkward because I was in and out of the kitchen and just saw bits, but that's how it was. For decorations, we had rolls of crêpe paper which the children made into different things and gradually we started collecting Christmas ornaments which I'm now giving back to the family as their families are growing.

Anne Dunkley

Christmas as a Married Woman

1958 was my first Christmas as a married woman in Hatfield. We were married in September and the house wasn't fully furnished. In those days you collected things as you went along. We had a put-you-up, and two armchairs given to us. We had a dining room suite and I was determined to have Christmas in my home. My sister and parents came and the couple my husband used to lodge with; who became surrogate grandparents to my children. We did have a chicken, because my father had been a butcher at one time in St Albans. People used to bring the chickens to him to kill and dress so I was always guaranteed a chicken. So we did have our bird on Christmas Day. I made my cake, I made my pudding, and I made my own mincemeat. Whether it was any good I don't know, but I was determined that this was what a married woman did and I was going to do it. We had a real Christmas tree. We did have electric lights which were from Woolworth's probably, and we started the collection of all our own things.

Barbara Latham

Christmas Didn't Start in August

Christmas didn't start in August as it appears to now. It was a fairly short and sharp affair. We came in the 1960s and our first Christmas was pretty sparse because our furniture hadn't come. We had a card table and two fold-up garden chairs, but we were determined that this was our house and we were going to have our Christmas. So we had a tree and everything that went with it and we cooked the meal etc. We went round to the in-laws on Boxing Day and subsequent days, but we were determined to have Christmas Day in our own home for the first time.

Jim Parker

Christmas Decorations

We had a Christmas tree and glass decorations. We used to hunt around when our parents were out, to see what we could find and under the bed we once found what we thought was going to be a work basket. We were very disappointed, but on Christmas morning there was a lovely treasure cot

HAVE YOUR NEW T.V. INSTALLED IN TIME FOR CHRISTMAS VIEWING

A LARGE SELECTION OF THE LATEST B3C 2 TRANSISTORISED T.V.s AVAILABLE FOR RENT OR PURCHASE.

FROM ONLY 8/3 PER WEEK

£8.5.0. deposit to comply with Government regulations. Nothing more to pay for 20 weeks.

Immediate installations. Home demonstrations arranged.

Personal attention to all your requirements.

A. L. YOUNG

HILLTOP SHOPPING CENTRE
HATFIELD 2608

A seasonal advertisement from 1965. This successful local business is still trading at Hilltop since opening there in 1958.

with a doll in it, which was much better. We didn't have our presents wrapped. My sister and I had little upholstered armchairs and when we came downstairs on Christmas Day there were our presents, all over the chairs. They were on the arms of the chair, behind it, so you walked in and you had the impact of all these little presents all over the place. Christmas Eve, my sister and I had to share the double bed in one room, because Aunty Flora came. She arrived with all her presents unwrapped and she locked herself in her room and all night she'd wrap presents. My sister and I, before we went to sleep on Christmas Eve, would have our own little carol concert in bed and then we'd say, 'I think I can hear sleigh bells.' This was when we were about eleven! On Christmas Day we had a large chicken or small turkey, we always had a bird.

Pat Lewis

The Christmas Tree

We moved into our house on 25 November 1955, exactly a month before Christmas Day. When it came to presents and such like, we had very little money and two boys; one was three and one was seven. I managed to get some old Dinky toys through Exchange and Mart, so I was working like blazes to paint them up and get them just right for Christmas and on Christmas Eve I was still painting some of them. As far as the Christmas tree went, what I did then, I had a big tin and I filled it with sand. I had a big piece of wood which I shaped, drilled holes in it diagonally, put coloured wire

through it at angles to make the branches and then tied it round with coloured paper. I was doing part – time electrical work as well so I managed to get hold of some fairy lights. They were in the style of Disney's Cinderella, which was popular at the time. I hung them on the tree and we had odds and ends for decorations. I worked in the retail trade, and the staff were able to keep the decorations that the firm no longer wanted from the previous year, so I could use those in my house. Another thing that stands out in my mind, is that we had a postal delivery on Christmas Day.

Ron Kingdon

Worried about the Needles

I worked on the children's ward in the QEII Hospital from 1965. The decorations there went up on Christmas Eve and they came down on Boxing Day. I remember people worrying about the needles on trees coming off the trees but you didn't have trees in the house until Christmas Eve to decorate and then they were finished so I don't think we ever realized the needles would fall anyway. Also the houses weren't that warm.

Jean Marshall

As a Treat we had Real Coffee

On Christmas Day, as a treat we had real coffee, you could buy ground coffee. We had a percolator for it, the vacuum thing, one on top of the other and it went up to the top, bubbled up and went down to the bottom.

Janet Vann

He Used to Think he'd Cooked it

There was a time when I worked at Wellfield Old People's Home and some of us had to work on Christmas Day. If I had to go to work I would get all the veg ready then I had an oven with a timer so I used to set it all so it started cooking. I only worked in the morning and my husband just kept an eye on it until I came home but he used to think he'd cooked it! It was nearly done when I got home.

Claire Figg

The Turkey

I think it must have been our first Christmas. The turkey had its feathers off but everything else was there and we had to take all the stuff out, and it said in Mrs Beeton that you had to pull the sinews on the legs. We lived in a flat in Meadowcroft then so we were outside trying to be as quiet as possible and trying to hang on to this beast. We tied it on the banisters and tried to pull it. Our opposite neighbour came out to see what we were doing. She was born and bred on a farm and she said, 'I'll show you what to do!'

David Dunkley

Girls at the Grammar School assembling their Christmas stained glass windows. Note the pleated skirts favoured by Pat Glanville's daughter. (*Welwyn and Hatfield Times*/Denis J. Williams)

Had to Put Your Name Down

In the old days Christmas didn't start until Christmas Eve. Now everybody seems to have mince pies and Christmas dinner beforehand so it's not such a treat on Christmas Day. We didn't have the birds all year so that's why you had to put your name down for one for Christmas

In the '50s and '60s we always seemed to be ordering turkeys long before Christmas. There was sometimes quite a long waiting list and if you were at the end you occasionally didn't get one. It seems

121

to have changed now, I never order one, we're very much more casual about it. I do remember on one occasion my father was at the end of the queue and he didn't get a turkey from the shop where he'd ordered it. He had to go out in the car round the farms of Hertfordshire to look for one. As most people were cooking their Christmas meal at about the same time, the gas would go down and this was frustrating when you were cooking the turkey.

Shirley Knapp

Lots of Turkey Thieves

I think we always had a turkey. We had a friend who had an uncle who had a turkey farm in Essex and David always used to go over and collect it. I locked myself into my bedroom on Christmas Eve and wrapped presents and David went off to get the Christmas turkey. It was the days when there were lots of turkey thieves and because he had a turkey in the back of the car, he was worried in case he got stopped by the police.

Anne Dunkley

Dr Burvill-Holmes (left), chairman of Hatfield Rural District Council, and Leslie Asquith, clerk of the RDC, at the switching-on of the White Lion Square Christmas lights, December 1964. (*Welwyn and Hatfield Times*/Denis J. Williams)

The Butcher was Open all Night

We didn't come here until 1966, but I remember from that time onwards the Co-op butcher at Hilltop on Christmas Eve being open all night while the staff plucked, dressed and cleaned the birds. They weren't anything like the ready fowl that there are now.

The Queen's Speech

We always had to listen to the Queen's Speech. It was a real tradition. We had to stand to attention when the National Anthem was played. We actually stood up. My father would have killed us by looks otherwise.

Christmas Visiting

I recall now that there was a considerable exodus from the New Town at Christmas. We didn't choose to go ourselves, but if I remember rightly, many of those around us, who had come from far afield, went 'home' as they still called it. But we were determined that this was our home and we were going to stay. I remember the whole estate became deserted almost; certainly for the first year.

Having People Round for Drinks

After we'd been here a few years with our Self Build Group, we used to start inviting people round for a drink on Christmas Eve but after a few years I was making food and it developed into a sort of party. We did that for years. Now I don't do it anymore but someone still does it. Before we had any children we used to always go up to Essendon. for a walk on Boxing Day.

Claire Figg

Carol Singing Until 2 a.m.

We moved to Hatfield in 1955 and eventually I discovered the group of Methodists meeting in the Roe Green area. When Christmas came it was decided to go carol singing. Several of the Church members were connected with Hatfield Technical College and there was a long list of people who would enjoy visits from carol singers. We would set off in the evening and sing in the roads near their houses. Every hour or so we would be invited into someone's house for mince pies and cups of tea and we would go on singing until about two in the morning. I used to go with the group each Christmas until I had our last baby.

Janet Vann

'Take the Next One!'

Our son was in the choir in St. Etheldreda's for a couple of years and at Christmas they used to have to go to Hatfield House to sing to the Salisbury family. The Salisbury younger children were all very smartly dressed and the choirboys were all given a gift off the Christmas tree. One year the gifts were paperbacks. When one of the choirboys was handed one, he said, 'I've

Hatfield and District British Rail Staff Association give a children's Christmas party at Cavendish Hall, December 1963. (*Welwyn and Hatfield Times*)

got that one,' and so they tried another one, and they said, 'What about this one?' The choir master said, 'Take the next one whatever it is!' That was about 1966 and our son was very impressed by the fact that the Salisbury grandchildren all wore Eton suits, striped trousers and black jacket.

Janet Vann

CHAPTER 11

End Thoughts

The Boomtime Group outside Hatfield Library. (Ken Wright)

A Victim of its Own Success?

Undoubtedly, Hatfield will not be the first town to become the victim of its own success, neither is it likely to be the last. Two major happenings were responsible for putting Hatfield on the industrial map. With the coming of the railway in 1850, Hatfield became a railway town. Seventy-plus years later Geoffrey de Havilland brought his manufacturing company to the district. With his foresight and enterprise in aeroplane design and construction, Hatfield and its aircraft industry became famous throughout the world with the factory creating the main source of employment for its inhabitants and others around. After World War Two, Hatfield was destined to become a new town with hundreds of new houses and a vast increase in population. The 1950s and '60s ushered in the 'Boomtime years'. Sadly, the next two decades saw far reaching changes taking place in the aircraft industry both in this country and abroad. This once great town, by relying mainly on one major concern to sustain the local economy found this to be its undoing.

Ron Kingdon

Hindsight

People, particularly people who don't do anything, are very good at giving advice to those that do, about what they should have done better. I suppose one can see a mistake in the upper tier of shops in the Town Centre, but it probably wouldn't have been if there had actually been more of them. The arrangement of the shops in the Town Centre is often criticized but as I say, you can criticize anything in hindsight, but the planners had a blank piece of paper and were trying to do something new. The construction in mainly concrete was cold, but that was the material of the time. I think we had some useful shops. We had some very useful dress shops for ladies, we had some good family grocers, butchers, and greengrocers; they provided good services. But I think Hatfield was developed at the time when people were beginning to get cars, and I wonder whether that wasn't part of the problem with Hatfield. People wanted to go elsewhere, look at other places, and to shop elsewhere. I think of the people who do the complaining about Hatfield, if they'd spent more of their money where they lived, they might still have more facilities than they have now.

Gerald Model

The Difference Cars have Made

I'm very struck by the difference cars have made to Hatfield. In the '50s and '60s people did most of their shopping locally. The children were in schools locally and they walked to school. The mums walked to the shops, to the clinic, and the libraries. Hilltop was a very busy area and there was a community spirit. It seems as though people now come out earlier on a Saturday, do their shopping quickly and possibly jump into their car and go off somewhere else. Whether they go to out of town supermarkets or whether they are off to do other things I'm not sure. It just seems that they don't stay in their local area on a Saturday any more.

Shirley Knapp

Walking was the Secret

The community spirit was there mainly due to the fact that before the car era people walked and talked and spoke to each other. When you're in a car you don't meet. You drive right down the road. You might wave but that's it. Walking was part and parcel of the community spirit.

A New Time with New Ideas

It all goes back to the idealism of the age. It was a new time with new ideas. People were still fired with that sort of attitude, they thought that man was perfectible, and that this new way of living was one way of perfecting him.

Donald Hodson

Anywhere but Hatfield

It is sad to me that my own children, now in their thirties down to twenty-four, don't want to live in Hatfield, want to move anywhere but Hatfield, but then of course, children do want to move away from where their parents live, that's fine. They find none of the excitement that I found living here, I have to say, they want to be in more absorbing communities.

David Cregan

How Exciting it Was

I felt the same, I remember how exciting it was when we first came here, and I felt there was a sort of pioneering spirit, and a lot of us are still here, possibly because of that.

Shirley Knapp

Thirty Years Later

There are a lot of people who say, 'We don't like Hatfield, we're going to move away', and thirty years later they're still here.

You Were Pioneers

People came from all over, so we were all starting, all new people came in. Their bookshelves were planks on bricks and they had newspaper up at the windows. We had a card table and two garden chairs as our first furniture. You were all starting as it were from scratch. I don't think anybody moved in with suites and chairs and tables. In those days you started building up and there was this feeling of helping out and you were pioneers in a way.

Jim Parker

Actually Building Something

I think what I miss is that feeling that everything you did in the town almost, even just going shopping, was a pioneering move of some sort. It was like Little House on the Prairie or something,

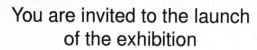

You are invited to the launch
of the exhibition

Boom Time : Hatfield
in the 1950s and 1960s

Monday 27th April 1998
3.00pm
Hatfield Library, Queensway, Hatfield

RSVP (01707) 263155

Project supported by

An invitation to the original Boom Time Project in 1998, from which this book evolved.

you were actually building something, even by just supporting a shop. Maybe that was just a fantasy but it's the thing I miss.

David Cregan

Starting Off from the Same Level

Whenever you go into a new project, whether it's at work or a new factory, or new place of employment, or a new estate, if you all go in together you seem to have that community spirit because you're all starting off from the same level.

Ron Kingdon

Hatfield and the North

When I am in London sometimes people ask, 'Where do you live?' and I say, 'Hatfield', and they say, 'There's this sign, "Hatfield and the North",' as if its all igloos up there. But I say 'Where do you live?' and they say, 'Wimbledon', and I say, 'How long does it take you to get home?', and they say, 'An hour and a half' whereas Hatfield is just twenty minutes up the line. There's that great advantage and the hospitals, all our children were born there, our grandchildren were born there. It's looked after us incredibly well!

David Cregan